RecruiterGuy's
GUIDE TO
FINDING A JOB

Bill Humbert
RecruiterGuy

RecruiterGuy's Guide to Finding a Job © Copyright 2010 by Bill Humbert.

Created and printed in the United States of America.

Published by the Corridor Media Group
845 Quarry Rd.
Coralville, IA 52241

ISBN 978-0-9828373-2-0

Library of Congress Cataloging-in-Publication Data
Control Number: 2010931925

The author and publisher assume no responsibility for errors, inaccuracies, omissions or any inconsistency herein.

First printing 2010

Editor: John Kenyon, Corridor Media Group
Design and layout: Jill Colbert, Corridor Media Group

For ordering information or special discounts for bulk purchases, please contact the Corridor Media Group at 845 Quarry Rd., Coralville, IA 52241 or (319) 887-2251. E-mail: info@corridorbiznews.com. Web: www.corridorbiznews.com.

For more information about the book or the author, contact Bill Humbert, 2025 Canyons Resort Dr. #U7, Park City, UT 84098 or (435) 649-0005. E-mail: recruiterguy@msn.com. Web: www.recruiterguy.com.

corridormedia**group**

FORWARD

Have you ever wanted to accomplish something few people have accomplished but put it off because you were too busy? Well, that was me until I committed myself to writing this book.

My experience is proof that once you commit yourself to accomplish something and take the necessary actions to be successful, you can succeed. Some people describe that as goal setting.

Thank you to my wife, Linda, and daughters Becky and Sarah. When you have the undying support of loved ones, you can accomplish anything.

Andrea — you have heard me tell many people that you were the best hire I ever made. It is still true. You worked with me through so many false starts on my books and always had great suggestions and supported my ideas. Thank you! Now it's your turn (wink, wink)!

Not to be forgotten are my parents, brothers and sisters. It's really cool how a family comes together and supports one another. Also, they have the relationship to ground you when needed — "Aw, he's just my brother..." Thank you!

Thanks to my elementary teachers in Chillum, Md. I still can diagram sentences and outline with the best of them! It just took me a while to season and put my thoughts on electronic paper.

Thanks to my teachers and guidance counselor John Moylan at DeMatha High School in Hyattsville, Md. Three teachers specifically made impacts in my life. Thanks to Father Mike who made biology fun while teaching it. I'll never forget the dead frog that flew out the window and landed on a student's car — I don't think anyone in my class ever parked under Father Mike's window again! Thanks to Buck Offutt who was an English teacher with few peers. Remember the Robin Williams movie when he was the teacher? The movie could have been based on Buck. He taught us not only how to comprehend what we were reading, but he taught us to think about what we were reading. Critical thinking is so important in our world! Thanks to Morgan Wootten. Some of you know Morgan as the result of his years of coaching basketball at DeMatha and the fact that he is in the Basketball Hall of Fame (2002). Morgan was my freshman homeroom teacher, my freshman history teacher (Yes, I still remember our project!) and a customer on my *Washington Post* paper route. Morgan taught us values and history — and the importance of not reliving it. He was a better history teacher than he was a basketball coach. Think about it... too bad there is not a History Teacher Hall of Fame!

My professors at Assumption College also contributed to this book because Assumption was my "finishing school." I learned a lot about life at Assumption. Isn't that one of the things you need to learn at that age? John Burke and Michael True were English professors who really made an impact in my life. I called John and told him that last month. I have to thank Larry Riordan, the admissions director who recruited me to Assumption and then gave me a work-study job in the admissions office. Who would have thought then that the seeds of my recruiting career were sown?

Special thanks go to Suzy Hanney of Park City, Utah. Early in the writing of this book, Suzy was kind enough to read the first few chapters. She suggested listing actions instead of positioning them in a paragraph format. This suggestion made my book easier to read and follow.

Be careful if you give a manuscript to Patti Seda, vice president of human resources at Yellow Book. She warned me that she loves to use her fine-toothed comb when reading a document. She did. And her comments were right on target. Many of Patti's suggestions were adopted in the final run of my manuscript. Patti, thank you for your time and suggestions!

A special thanks to Joe Patten. He has been a friend, mentor and client since 1996. His suggestions helped me develop a stronger, more relevant book.

I've heard that many authors must send a manuscript to many publishers before one agrees to publish the book. I sent my introduction and first three chapters to John Lohman at Corridor Media

Group and he agreed that my book may have some merit. Talk about propelling me to finish it! Thanks, John! John Kenyon found the rough edges and massaged them so it would be easier for the reader. Jill Colbert did an outstanding job designing the cover and inside feel of my book. Books are a team effort. Thank you!

Finally, thank you to God (by whatever name)! This book was written to help other people. You kept your promise!

- Bill Humbert

RecruiterGuy's Guide to Finding a Job

Introduction

Appendix A: List of Action Verbs and Phrases for Executives,
Mid-Career and Entry-Level Candidates

Appendix B: Potential Interview Questions for Which to Prepare

INTRODUCTION

My business is RecruiterGuy.com. Many times since the early 1990s, when I am in client offices, people greet me as "RecruiterGuy."

I come by that title honestly. I became a professional recruiter in 1981. As a contingent recruiter (fee-based "head hunter") in Washington, D.C., I specialized in recruiting IT professionals (back then we called them data-processing professionals).

In 1990, I started a contract recruitment consulting firm, The Humbert Group. The focus was different from the contingent business model. The focus instead is on one company at a time to provide recruitment process improvement, recruitment strategy development, recruitment web site search engine optimization and to train managers how to recruit "impact performers."

The RecruiterGuy.com web site was developed in 2001 to provide resources for companies, candidates and other recruiters.

Finally, during the economic and jobs recession of 2008-10, RecruiterGuy.com, a nationally based recruitment consulting firm, was moved from Iowa to the business-friendly state of Utah.

What is the common denominator? In 1981, I began recruiting during what was then the worst recession since World War II. During the next recession of 1990, I started my own recruitment firm. During the recession of 2001, I developed my web site — www. RecruiterGuy.com. Finally, during the recession of 2008, I moved my business to Utah. My actions prove that I can make major changes during recessions — and so can you! **Remember, if unemployment is 10 percent, employment is 90 percent. Work to become one of the 90 percent who are employed.**

Since 1981, I have worked with thousands of managers and candidates and have voluntarily helped hundreds of people find their next position — even in recessions. Beginning in late August 2009, RecruiterGuy and three other volunteer professionals organized the Park City Career Network. By March 2010, 25 of our members found positions in their fields during one of the worst employment markets in years, and 10 of our members started small businesses. The search process works — if you faithfully work it.

In my experience doing volunteer career counseling, I see the frustration of jobseekers going through the search process. Because I have helped so many people find their next job, it seemed time to write a book that assists the jobseeker to understand the processes involved and helps them to be more successful. The processes in this book can be used by anyone — from a C-level executive to a college recruit.

Fundamentals are fundamentals; higher-level professionals simply have higher-level experience, expectations, skills and contacts, and a slightly different path to their next job. The salary-negotiating tool in this book benefits executive-level candidates more than others because they have more leverage. One executive who accepted a president position with a company happily reported that my tool enabled him to accept an offer that was 40 percent above what he expected the company to offer and 20 percent above what he was going to request.

Think about your search for your first job. Did someone sit down with you and prepare you for your search? Did you take a class? If you were in college and someone from the career development department tried to help you prepare for your search, did you take them seriously?

When do many people initially learn how to find a job? When they are in high school or college and a parent suggested they needed to find a job. What did most people do in that situation? They applied for a part-time position at the grocery, in retail or a fast food restaurant — and got their first job. If they were successful in those early positions, they may have been recruited to join another company. This was followed up by being recruited to do their next job — and they are well into their career without truly working through a job search.

People tend to repeat actions that worked for them previously in a given situation. When they begin a job search, they try to repeat the actions that worked for them in the past. When the situation becomes desperate, they depend more on that previous successful behavior. This is the foundation for behavioral interviewing. The job-search problem that occurs for most people is that the process changes after their first job or after they have been recruited for a number of jobs; therefore, they do not have a successful process to fall back on.

Pay attention to the next sentence: The job-search process is a combination of several processes. This is very important to remember.

This book has been organized by process so you can pick it up at any time and review chapters that affect your situation. Do not read this book from front to back like a novel. Use it as a reference to help you work through each process. Each process has its place, and each process is important to do well. These are the processes that you will work through on the way to successfully finding your next job:

- Your psychological acceptance process if you were laid off or otherwise feel betrayed by your last employer or board
- Deciding your next direction or focus, and setting a goal to achieve it
- The resume-development process (For some of us that truly is a work in progress!)
- The research/networking process (sourcing/prospecting in sales)
- The interviewing process (needs analysis in sales)
- The offer/salary negotiation process
- The offer acceptance process
- The on-boarding process when you accept the company's offer and start working

Is it any wonder that people are frustrated when they look for their next professional position, particularly if they were loyal to their first employer for 10, 20 or more years? The same process they used to find their first position does not work for their next search — outside of retail. If they have been with an employer for 20 or more years and were laid off, they feel deceived and betrayed. Those feelings are so strong they are almost like a concussion — everything becomes a blur. Then the company, while truly trying to help them, will sometimes introduce them to outplacement assistance for a certain amount of time. This help occurs while a person is still trying to grasp what happened, so little of what they are taught sticks. Once they get their emotions back under control, outplacement assistance may be a great help.

Other people really never had to look for their next position. They were working hard and making an impact with their current company and, as a result, they were approached by another company or recruited by a professional recruiter. Their career proceeded nicely that way until they found themselves out of work. Now they find themselves starting from the beginning for the first time in years.

When you look at the job-search process as a series of smaller important processes, you can understand why so many books have been written on different aspects of the search. **Now it is easier to see why so many people are frustrated during a job search. They think they are "just looking for a job."**

Treat your job search as work. It is hard work. The search is worth it if you find a job where you can make positive, measurable impacts and have fun doing so — in other words, one that makes you happy. My desire is that you are successful finding a job you enjoy so much that at the end of each day you say to yourself, "I enjoyed myself so much today, I can't believe they are actually paying me to do this!"

This book has been developed to help you understand the processes and begin the day-to-day steps to be successful. Lao Tzu said, "A journey of 1,000 miles begins with a single step." It is time for you to take the first step. I will help you. If you fall down, go back to the last point where you were successful and begin again. You can do it. Believe it or not now, your successes will lift you.

A CFO who is conducting his or her search will need to focus on different aspects of the process than a new college graduate. A new college graduate generally is not going through the emotional trauma as someone who recently lost a job. Feel free to scan through areas that do not directly impact you. Focus on the different tasks within each process and use the checklists at the end of each chapter to stay on track. Use a bookmark to return to chapters where you are working.

You have seen and heard the legal stuff before. Here is mine: There are too many variables for me to make guarantees, and no legal advice is given in this book. If you need legal advice, go to an attorney in your town or state.

CHAPTER 1
OUR FIRST STEPS TOGETHER

If you are perusing this chapter, you are probably one of millions of people who are in the midst of a job search or considering a search. The key is to become one of the tens of millions of people who are employed. You only need one position where you can make impacts and have fun — don't focus on the negative numbers. Focus on finding one job. Those who are most successful in their job searches are the ones who maintain a positive attitude and perform the fundamentals like winning athletes.

The purpose of this book is to coach you so that you understand and work the fundamentals of a job search so well that you become the best-qualified candidate for the right job. You are competing against other well-qualified candidates who may not understand these processes. You will need to focus and remain positive.

Just as in athletics and the performing arts, the people with the right attitudes, work ethic and proper techniques beat their competition. Job-search fundamentals are essentially the same if you are a CEO/CFO, a midlevel manager or sole contributor; a technology, accounting/finance or a sales/marketing professional; an entry-level candidate or a student seeking an internship or co-op. Different areas of this book focus on each level of experience.

When I offer career counseling to people, many times they seem to be afraid to take that first step into the unknown — the uncomfortable new territory; however, after they begin to experience some success, the adrenalin kicks in and they become comfortable with that area, but maybe not the next new area.

It is important to understand that it is not unusual for people

to find change uncomfortable. As humans, many of us do not like change. Our society has been built through the years to be stable. Stability and change are opposing forces; therefore, our goal here is to help you work your way through change to get back to stability.

When you lose a job or the forces within a job become so unbearable that you decide to leave (or your spouse decides that the job is so bad for you that you become unbearable!), you will need to work through the steps of grief acceptance.

The feeling of grief occurs when you lose someone or something close to you. For instance, if you lose a close family member, or even a pet, you will experience grief. When we lost our beloved 13-and-a-half-year-old Labrador Retriever (If you read *Marley and Me* by John Grogan, you knew our Kiefer) immediately after the 2010 Grammys (she hung around to see who won album of the year), we found ourselves working through the steps of grief: denial and disbelief, anger, depression and acceptance.

When you lose a job that you loved or maybe just worked at for a long time, you will need to work your way through the steps of grief. Some people really do not have a problem doing this. They may be able to embrace change more easily. If your job becomes your identity, you typically will have a more difficult time reaching acceptance. If there is any good news, it is that you have lots of company — and I have met many people in your work shoes. You may think that you are over the anger or depression. Then, just when you expected to receive an offer, you are turned down for that position. The rejection may send you backwards into a previous step of grief. I've known people who felt like they never were going to get beyond their grief. They kept circling one or another step like they were in a whitewater hole in a river. They sometimes simply felt hopeless; however, just as in whitewater rafting, if you focus and work really hard, eventually you will be kicked out of the hole and continue down the river of life.

If you find either your anger or your depression beginning to take control over you, it is time to get some professional help. Just understand, there is no stigma attached to getting professional help; however, if you do something out of control, there is a stigma (or worse) attached to those actions.

Remember that you will go through all of those steps. There is no timeline to reach acceptance. Every person is different.

Your departure from your former employer may not have been your fault, but if it was, it is best just to admit it to yourself and move on to your next step. Most of us have experienced denial and disbelief during a loss. For some people, one or another of the steps will be easier.

If you would like to read more on the steps (or stages) of grief, go to www.google.com and search for "steps of grief."

While working your way through the stages of grief, this is the time to begin to develop your job-search strategy. RecruiterGuy suggests that you take advantage of this early stage by taking stock of your skills. Some counselors call this a skills assessment.

Take two legal sheets. On the top of one sheet write the word "Professional." You need to use a legal sheet because it has more lines. On each line, write one of your skills or attributes. An example of a skill for a midlevel manager is the ability to manage people effectively. It may also be something as simple as the ability to organize a desk drawer. Examples of attributes are honesty and positive mental attitude. Another example is a winning personality. Fill at least every line on the front page with a skill or attribute.

Once you are satisfied with your "Professional" list, write the word "Personal" on the top of the second legal sheet. List all of your personal skills and attributes. I once worked with a very talented network engineer who baked absolutely world-class desserts. We loved to see him walk into our office with his latest baked deliciousness! This network engineer would need to include that skill in his personal list. It doesn't matter how seemingly silly the skill or attribute is — list it. One of my skills is that I make the best spaghetti in Park City, Utah. (So obviously you can't use that one in Park City!)

Some skills and attributes will straddle both lists. It's fine to place them on both.

Now go back through both lists and put asterisks next to the skills and attributes that you enjoy doing. For instance, as a human resource consultant specializing in the recruitment area, one of my skills is the ability to be very effective with employee relations issues.

However, this is neither enjoyable nor fun for me; therefore, it does not earn an asterisk.

Once you have placed asterisks next to skills and attributes, develop a quick discussion of a situation that required each skill. Discuss what you did as a result of the situation. Then discuss what happened as a result of your influence or direct action for each skill or attribute that demonstrates your ability. Just stating that a skill or attribute is a strength is not a metric. My kneejerk reaction is, "As compared to what?" Besides, people remember stories better than lists because we put ourselves into the story and relive it with you. While you are telling your story, we are picturing the events as though we were there.

One of my skills as RecruiterGuy is to be very resourceful. In August 2008, I began a recruiting consulting contract with Acciona Energy NA, a renewable energy company. This was the first time in 27 years of recruitment that I was supporting a construction function within a client company. Within three weeks, I set up five personal interviews on-site and my client hired three of those candidates for three positions we had open. How was I successful so quickly? I used the skills that I developed and honed over the years to source candidates, and applied them to this new field. In the process, I discovered a new job board for my client to use in future construction candidate searches.

It is best that you are prepared going into an interview having already dredged up the best stories that demonstrate your abilities. Most of your competitors will not prepare this way.

Why is this exercise important? There are a number of reasons why you need to be serious about this work:

- You need to review these skills and attributes to prepare yourself for your interviews.

- You need to be able to demonstrate that these are measurable skills.

- It is important for you to understand your value to a new

company.

- This exercise helps you through the other stages of grief and may be enough to propel you through them. These stories create the foundation to renew your self-worth.
- You may decide that this is a great time to go in a completely different career direction where you are using the skills you really enjoy — possibly even starting your own business. Have fun at work. What a concept!

I once was interviewed for a presentation on "Effective Networking to Your Next Position!" The freelance writer honored me by telling me that two years before, she was going through a particularly tough job search. We spoke after one of my presentations. During our conversation, we discussed the job-search process and aspects of it that she had not considered. As a result of our conversation, she changed her search completely and now is enjoying her new career in sales. She is now using the same relationship-building skills that she had been previously, but in a way that is more fun and generates more income.

Place a book marker in this page and complete the task of developing stories that demonstrate your skills before continuing further.

It is important in the early stages of a job search to be task-focused. Every task completed is a success. Right now, success in any process is important to your self-worth and helps you build a positive attitude. As we move forward, the processes will require more strategic skills and sometimes multitasking.

Many times, once you get past your denial, you find yourself angry at your situation, your job loss, your former manager, your former company and/or executives, yourself or all of the above. Anger is fine if you work through it. Revenge can be a strong motivator; however, the revenge needs to be directed toward a positive conclusion, not toward an individual or company. Be careful with revenge because it can become all-encompassing. Use its power to find your next job where you can make positive, measurable impacts. Then, when you are wildly successful at your next company, you can briefly look back and say to yourself, "See!"

Obviously, this is the time to work on more positive activities to prepare for networking. You will need to know whom to call and their phone numbers. This gives you a track to work every day. With the ease of creating spreadsheets and expanding them as needed, I recommend that you create a spreadsheet with four columns: name, phone number, where the person works and how you know him or her (This may be a referral from someone else). You can also use paper or even a whiteboard.

List 250 names in those spreadsheets. It seems like a lot of names and phone numbers. But when you begin to network, you will need at least that many contacts. They do not need to be friends. The list may contain family, friends, acquaintances, pastor/rabbi/minister/ spiritual mentor, parents of your children's friends, former peers at other companies, former managers, alumni from your high school and college(s), your banker, attorney and real estate agents. Ask your family to look at your list. They may remember people that you forgot. You do not have to create this list in one sitting. As a matter of fact, it is good practice to add to it consistently.

If you are a CEO, CFO, CTO, CIO, CMO, CHRO, etc., your list needs to contain the names of consultants or account executives that have sold or tried to sell you their products or services. Obviously, these people have connections to people in your field at your level. Depending upon their products or services, they may know influential corporate board members.

If you are an experienced manager or sole contributor, your list should contain friends who are in sales, previous peers and managers, as well as former classmates from high school and college. All of these people know other people and may be influential in helping you meet the right person.

If you are graduating from college and are new to the workforce, you also have access to a network of names in the workforce. Attend the on-campus and local career fairs. Contact people where you worked on an internship. Have you discussed your search with your friends? Do you know what their parents' professions are?

If you have not already created a profile on www.LinkedIn.com and have begun inviting people you know to your LinkedIn network, you need to begin working on that now. You can find people listed by companies and by educational affiliations (high schools and colleges). You can also join LinkedIn groups that are tied to your industry and associations that are tied to your fields. LinkedIn has become a very valuable tool for both business development and job searching. There is more information on LinkedIn in Chapter 4 Effective Networking to Your Next Position!

Networking to a Job spreadsheet (sample)

Name	Phone	Company	How known
John Doe	435-555-2045	Ability Co.	Neighbor
Jane Doe	435-555-2391	Honest Insurance	Neighbor
Irving Milliken	319-555-9345	Accountant Inc.	Jane Doe

Before proceeding to the next task, really focus on developing your list of names. This list is very important for tracking and setting goals for your networking activities. **You need the base of 250 names because "warm" referrals are your most valuable commodity during a job search.** If you can list 500 names of potential contacts, you will regain confidence and accelerate your job search. Additionally, when a contact is one of 500, there is less pressure on you to get some kind of results from that person. Then you are more relaxed in your conversation with them. The practice of exceeding expectations works in jobs and in job searches.

Once you work your way through your anger, you may find yourself depressed. Many times the loss of a job brings feelings that you are somehow worthless. Just understand that companies do not have good track records when it comes to laying off the right people. You may have been an "impact performer" in the wrong place at the wrong time. Again, if you cannot work through depression by yourself, seek professional help. Just understand that many people experience depression during this process. You are not alone in these feelings. Generally, many people cry while they are discussing their feelings with me. My reaction is that it is important to let them cry. It can help them work their way through their situation — kind of a cleansing. Once the crying is done, it's back to work with a sense of urgency.

Given the practice of promoting positive activity during negative times, if you find yourself in a funk because of your situation, now is the time to begin to list your accomplishments over the past five years. This list is different than the skills assessments in that you are focused on your professional impacts. If you are feeling depressed, it may be difficult to develop a list of accomplishments. That is not at all unusual. Why? It is difficult for our minds to switch from negative to positive — and from positive to negative. This is the reason you need to focus on a positive activity when you do not feel positive. Focus on positive results to work through the negative feelings.

Accomplishments in former positions can be large money-saving endeavors or smaller achievements. A sales professional may have the accomplishment of exceeding quota for the past three years. An operations leader in manufacturing may have used Lean processes to lower costs and increase productivity. A commercial banker may have several years when every loan was profitable and closed on time.

For practice, use action verbs to describe the activity. Never begin an accomplishment with the words "have or had." **Always begin a resume sentence with an action verb** (See Appendix A). There are also lists of action verbs on the Internet, so simply type "action verbs" into a search engine like Google or Bing to find potential verbs that fit your experience. **Here are some examples: designed, developed, managed, created, saved, solved, recruited, mentored, piloted, audited, introduced, negotiated, motivated, purchased, analyzed, assessed and organized.**

This is an example of one of my accomplishments. As the recruiting manager of a startup telecommunications firm, I discovered that our paper process to open new jobs was unwieldy. We were too dependent on people staying at their desks to approve the openings. Additionally, we never knew where jobs were in the approval process. I noticed that our help desk professional was using Lotus Notes shareware to develop applications for our customer service group.

Because applications are the automation of paper process, I approached the help desk professional to ask if she would be interested in teaming to develop an automated process to track job requisitions. She said she was interested. I then approached her manager to get his approval for her to work on this project during her unproductive time.

We worked on this project part-time over six months. She did a great job! We ended up developing an applicant-tracking system/human resource information system in 1995 using Lotus Notes shareware. It did not cost our startup any money. The system was robust enough to be used as the company grew from 400 employees to 8,000.

A positive mental attitude is crucial during a job search. In his book *How to Stop Worrying and Start Living*, Dale Carnegie had wonderful advice. Ask yourself, "What is the worst possible outcome of this situation? Once that is on the table, work to improve on it." This is a great book and one worth reading, especially if you are feeling stressed. It helped me through a particularly tough patch early in my recruitment career.

It is generally good to find something positive to do during this period while you are angry or depressed. Have you considered volunteering? This is a great outlet. It gets you out of the house. You are meeting people, contributing with your skills and sometimes helping people who are in a much worse position than you are. Generally, the people who receive the benefit of your service are genuinely grateful for everything that you do. These positive actions reinforce your sense of worth and give back to your community.

Who do we find on the boards of nonprofits? Usually, business people accept those positions. It's a great way to get noticed and at the same time feel more worthwhile. Doing something that is positive is far more productive than sitting at home depressed. When we discuss networking, your volunteer work is a great base because you are demonstrating that you are not only concerned about yourself, you are also concerned about others. It also gives you possible discussion points during interviews. And remember your contacts? It adds names to your list.

Occasionally, I have seen people have such a great experience in their volunteer work that they decide to accept a position with the nonprofit and they make contributions to its success as a full-time employee.

Finally, you reach the acceptance stage. It won't be a flash, but you will know when you get there. It simply will be the recognition that now is the time to move forward in a positive direction. Once you reach acceptance, it is time to get out and prepare to interview.

Congratulations!

Now you are in a positive position to take the next steps. Let's move forward and treat this search like your job. Get up in the morning. Take a shower. Dress professionally as you did for work — or possibly more professionally as a consultant or sales professional. You need to work at least eight hours every day on some aspect of your search, including volunteer work. RecruiterGuy will continue to help you take each day at a time.

Let's review your "TO-DO LIST" before moving on:

❑ Take stock of your skills in your professional and personal lives **using Descriptive Impact Verbs** (Refer to Appendix A).

❑ Develop a quick discussion of the situation that required each particular skill. Discuss what you did as a result of the situation. Then discuss what happened as a result of your influence or direct action for each skill or attribute that demonstrates your skill. **People remember stories, not lists.**

❑ **Develop a list of your positive, measurable impacts.** Develop a situation-action-result around each impact, and what you learned. If you still have old annual reviews, read through them for impacts that you may have forgotten.

❑ **Develop a list of a minimum of 250 names of family, friends and acquaintances,** neighbors, former peers/managers in your last company and previous companies, high school and college alumni, pastor/rabbi/spiritual mentor, banker, attorney and real estate agents. Look up their contact information in your address book, the phonebook or search for them with Google or Bing on the Internet.

❑ Join LinkedIn and invite everyone you feel can help you and that you can help somewhere. Remember, it is important to give back to other people. When people accept your invitation, go through their network and see if there may be contacts that you forgot to enter on your list. This action may help you remember additional people to add to your spreadsheet. Remember that people know other people — and LinkedIn is a great example of how it can work.

Now it's time to work on your next step. Remember to focus on each step and do it well. Then you can move to the next step or process. Some processes will take longer than others. It is good to use the above list to check off completed steps. You are building a strong foundation that will improve your job search.

Work very hard to maintain a positive mental attitude. You attitude will determine how quickly you find a job. Remember Winston Churchill during the darkest hours of the Battle of Britain in World War II — "Neva Give Up!"

Remember your bookmark? This is a great place to use it if you need to complete these tasks.

Let's get started on "What's Next? Here I Am!"

CHAPTER 2
WHAT'S NEXT? "HERE I AM!"

Think of your search as a new adventure. Enjoy your hunt! Don't get swallowed up in the perceived enormity of your search for your new job. Simply stay focused on your very next task. As you are successful in each task, you are moving in the direction of success to reach your final goal — a new job or possibly even starting your own business using the skills that you enjoy.

Since 1994, when I have spoken to organizations nationwide on the "Secrets of a Successful Job Search," I asked those gathered the following question: "What elements make you happy when you are working?" Generally, there are many responses, including compensation or benefits. Think about it. There are many elements that can make you happy — great peers, great managers, fun projects, great benefits/pay, cool challenges, self-fulfillment, etc. When you boil all of these down to the base elements, what are the things that combine with others to make you happy? Doesn't it come down to, "Am I making positive, measurable impacts?" and "Am I having fun doing so?"

If you are making positive, measurable impacts and having fun doing so, you will make the impacts necessary to earn what you need. So the feeling that I would love to see you achieve at work is this: "I am making such great impacts and having so much fun, I can't believe they are paying me, too!" You can reach that level of satisfaction. Along with the work to find your new position, this is the theme that is interwoven throughout this book. If you are conducting a job search, why not find something that you love to do — and be paid well to do it?

Let's review where you should be now in your search. You are probably three to five days into your search while reading this book. You have completed your skills assessments, probably even made some additions to your skills and attributes after chatting with people you know. Sometimes others can see things in you that you don't recognize until they point them out; therefore, it is good to ask other people for their feedback.

You worked a little on the list of examples that demonstrate successful use of those skills, but gave up after awhile because you were frustrated that you are in this situation and are anxious "to get started." Remember, this is a process. To win championships, individuals or teams need to perform the fundamentals well. How do they perform the fundamentals well? They practice them to perfection every single day. Chances are that you may have never worked on some of these fundamentals during job searches. Let's practice and do them well!

I have voluntarily helped hundreds of people succeed in finding their next job through this process. Have you ever snow skied? When you were learning how to ski, did you immediately go to the expert slopes? Probably not. You worked your way up to them. It was a process that involved success and failure. The successes built your confidence to try the next, more difficult slope. That's the process we are growing here. Build some success somewhere. Use that new confidence to go to the next step. **Remember, a positive mental attitude is crucial in the job-search process.**

Going back to your skills assessment, it is very important to develop the examples that demonstrate your success with that skill or attribute. After jotting down some examples, get away from them overnight. The next morning, you may remember better examples for some of those skills or attributes. During the interviewing process, I refer to them as the "Wish I Would Have Saids!" So write enough down that you will remember them.

All of this is important preparation prior to your interviewing process, so focus on doing the best job you can. Your search success, income and happiness depend on it. You will notice that occasionally I will reinforce process tasks that I mentioned in previous chapters.

I do this because of my experience working with people. It's not unusual to get further down the road while career counseling and have someone tell me, "Well, I really haven't focused on that yet…" **Think of RecruiterGuy as the little guy sitting on your shoulder in a business suit, with legs dangling and rooting you on — and whispering in your ear that you need to do a better job on your list of potential networking names or skills or accomplishments.**

You began your list of 250 people and then gave up after the first 53 names because it seemed like there were too many names to dredge up. Most people have impacted the lives of 250 people in some fashion, so ask your immediate family who you've forgotten from your list and add them. Did you remember your friends and acquaintances in your neighborhood? How about neighbors in former neighborhoods? If both members of a couple are working, you can add both names. (Never assume that married/significant other couples talk about everything!) Where have you volunteered? Who do you remember from those experiences? What sales professionals do you know? They truly understand the networking process. Their livelihoods depend on networking. Go to your high school and college alumni associations and see who you forgot to add from there. Remember that it's not just your class; you knew people in the classes before you and after you. You have your high school and college in common with them. Generally, people still feel warmth toward others who had similar experiences, whether in school or work. That is the reason you see work alumni groups on LinkedIn. We are now focusing on your "warm" contacts who have something in common with you.

While you are working on those tasks, I have another question that I ask during my "Secrets of a Successful Job Search" presentation. How many of you, in some part of your life, are involved in sales? If you agree, raise your hand. Invariably a few people will not raise their hand. So I suggest that I was not asking if they made their living in sales. The key phrase is "in some part of your life." I ask again, "How many of you, in some part of your life, are involved in sales?" Upon reflection, more people raise their hand.

There is always that one person who insists they are not involved in sales. So

I ask them, "Have you ever tried to sell a child on the idea of finishing their meal or going to bed?" They shake their head "No." So I ask them if they ever tried to sell a friend on the idea of going to a ball game, movie or other activity. They still say, "No." So I persist nicely and ask if they have ever tried to sell a co-worker on a better way to do things? Generally, they have gone this far down the path and don't want to admit they are wrong so they say, "No."

Then I ask, "So what I am hearing (pause) is that you are trying to sell me on the idea that you are not involved in sales, is that correct?" Everyone else thanks their lucky stars that they raised their hand.

The process to find a job is a sales process. People who realize this are successful more quickly than those who don't. The good news is that we have gotten you this far before we had to tell you this information — and you have built some belief and success through your early tasks, if you completed them.

Now that it is documented that you are in a sales process, let's treat it as such. One of the first things new sales professionals are taught is how to set and attain goals.

Decide on your next career and set a goal. When you are setting goals, it is important to consider all of the elements of a goal. I recommend that you use the word **SCAMPS** to remember the elements:

S – Specific: Your goal needs to be specific in order for you to visualize successfully reaching your goal.

C – Challenging: Challenging goals spur you to action. You are excited to work on them.

A – Attainable: While they need to be challenging, you must also believe that you can successfully attain them. Otherwise you will not work to succeed.

M - Measurable: The steps to completing a goal must be measurable. It is important to know every day the steps that you need to take toward achieving your goal. If the goal is not measurable, how will you determine your required tasks?

P – Public: You need to let people who support you know that you set the goal. They will ask for progress reports. This provides accountability.

S – Set Date: Once you have created a goal, it is important to set your completion date. This step, tied to the measurable steps enables you to determine what actions you need to take daily in order to achieve your goal.

In your job search, your goal could be, "By Jan. 2 (or whatever the date is 90 days out), I will be working as a(n) _____. I will get this position by contacting at least 20 new networking contacts per week to discuss my background." This is a realistic goal as long as the position could be available by then. You also are giving yourself a way of measuring your activity.

Nothing irritates me more while working a career fair than when a candidate approaches me and says, "So what do you have open?" My response always is the same: "What do you want to do?" When you are in the midst of a job search, it is important to be able to verbalize your job-search goal. Don't fear rejection.

It's time for the bookmark again. Take some time to internalize what I just said and develop your first goals. One of your goals might be to complete the tasks that have already been assigned within the next two days. If you begin having success, it is fine to set more aggressive goals — just be realistic and understand that more aggressive goals require more aggressive work and results.

Let us now work on your list of accomplishments in your jobs over the past five years. You have already listed your skills and attributes and developed stories that demonstrate success using them. You created your accomplishment list. Now list the most recent accomplishments first and the earlier accomplishments further down the list. Put them in the descending order of accomplishing them. If you still have employee reviews, you can use them to jog your memory. If you were very astute, you may have developed a list of your accomplishments every year prior to your annual review.

Now that we have much of the preparation done, the process will move more quickly. Hopefully you have made some progress working through the steps of grief — watch out for that denial one! When I hear someone protest they are not in denial when I did not even bring it up in our conversation, should I feel they may still be in denial? My sense is, "yes."

Because we are in a sales process, now we are going to work on the first of your marketing pieces — your "Here I Am!" speech. It's time to get your creative juices flowing and have some fun with this task. Your "Here I Am!" speech is also called an elevator speech or one-minute commercial. This is the beginning of branding yourself as a candidate or professional. The more successful candidates are the ones who do a good job differentiating themselves. Your "Here I Am!" speech is not something you can memorize; it is something you feel. You'll know you have hit it on the head when it feels good to you when you repeat it.

Let's work on building it right now. **What are the base elements of a "Here I Am!" speech?**

- **Talk about your experience and talents/impacts.** It's important to discuss why you are passionate about that type of work. That is a key differentiator for you.

- **Discuss briefly why you are in this situation of looking for a job.** Relax. My feeling is that the recession in the early 1990s was the first white-collar recession. The dot-bomb recession from 2000 to 2002 was strongly a professional and technical recession. Then the recession of 2008 until 2011 impacted everyone; therefore, everyone knows someone who was laid off or otherwise lost a job and did not deserve to be out of work.

- **Talk about what you would like to do next.**

This is an example of a "Here I Am!" speech that an engineer gave me after 9/11 when his company had to lay off several thousand professionals.

"When I was a kid, my dad was an air traffic controller and private pilot. He had his own plane. Every weekend, we would go up in the plane. My dad put me in his lap as he flew the plane, and I pretended to be the pilot. When I was older, I set a goal to get my pilot's license at the same time I passed my driver's license. When I was 16 years old, I earned both. When I graduated from high school, I went into the Air Force and began working on avionics equipment as a tech. Eventually, the Air Force promoted me to an avionics engineer. After I left the Air Force, I became an avionics engineer for (avionics company). As a matter of fact, if you are a (major airline) pilot flying a 767-400, I created the menu for the flat-panel display and determined when objects appeared in that display — so you are flying a plane with the menu I created. As a result of 9/11, (avionics company) had to lay off 3,000 people and I was one of them. Now I would like to go to work for another avionics company where I can help make flying safer for the pilots and the people they fly."

Do you feel the passion in his "Here I Am!" speech? Two weeks after he created his differentiator, he had an offer from another avionics company. That is how important your "Here I Am!" speech is. It needs to be sincere and passionate about what you have done and desire to do. Include a major accomplishment in your discussion. It is the beginning of your brand. It needs to be memorable for the person hearing it. They don't need to be able to repeat it. They need to remember it. Why? Many times when managers are actively interviewing many candidates, they forget names and details; however, they remember stories. *I have repeatedly heard managers say, "I don't remember his name. They were the one that told the story about..." Suddenly the other managers chime in and one of them remembers the name.*

It's time for the bookmark again. Take time to focus on your "Here I Am!" speech. Start to develop it. This usually is a task that takes a couple of days to hone. Remember, it must come from your heart. Trying to memorize it will fail because you can't memorize passion, you feel it. You know you have it when you can give it to a friend with total confidence and feel the passion in your branding.

Now that you are differentiating yourself and developing a brand for yourself, it is important to keep your brand consistent. It may evolve, and probably will as you interview and learn more about the requirements of the managers and companies where you are interviewing. Your "Here I Am!" speech and LinkedIn profiles need to be similar. Include aspects of your "Here I Am!" speech in your LinkedIn profile.

It's time for your progress review:

- By now, you recognize that you are involved in a sales process and as a result have completed your skills assessment with examples that demonstrate success with those skills and attributes.

- You have written at least 226 names on your list of warm contacts (family, friends and acquaintances). You are working on the other 150 to 250 names (good that you are exceeding expectations!). How about former professors? Doctors? People you met at the health club or during social events?

- You have listed your accomplishments, beginning with the most recent and working backward.

- You have developed your "Here I Am!" speech. Practice it with people you know well first. It can be as simple as "Hey, I am working on a differentiator for my candidacy. Would you mind listening to it as I practice?" Most people would love to help you.

- Now you are developing your brand as a candidate. Our next step is to tie everything together in your resume. The combination of resume, LinkedIn profile and "Here I Am!" speech are your primary marketing preparations for networking and then interviewing.

Now it is time to get started on your primary marketing piece — your resume!

CHAPTER 3
DEVELOPING YOUR
MARKETING PIECE — YOUR RESUME

For every foot between New York and California, there has been a book written about writing your resume. You may have already noticed this on Amazon.com or Barnes & Noble. Some were written by people who are writers. Some were written by people who saw a chance to use some common sense and make some money. Others were written by professionals in the business. Obviously, in a book discussing the entire job-search process, I (in the recruitment business since 1981) cannot go into the detail a book on resumes alone would give; however, we can go over the basics to help you get back to work. Over the years, I have read more than 400,000 resumes and have seen some resumes that are truly classics. You will hear about some of them in this chapter.

Occasionally, a candidate wants to demonstrate his creativity. When word processing first became popular, one candidate decided to create a box around his name and contact information. Unfortunately, he created a shaded box that covered the information. He could not have even looked at it before sending it out! I did not call, but I imagined my call to his company: "Hey, who is the programmer at your company who used to work at ABCD Company?"

One of the most important fundamentals to understand is that the recruiting process is a sales process. We discussed this concept in the previous chapter and I will repeat it again in future chapters. In the

RecruiterGuy presentations on the recruitment process from both sides of the desk, I subtitle the presentation, "Recruiting is Sales." Something else that few people understand is that the job search is a combination of several processes.

If the recruitment process is a sales process, then your resume is your marketing piece. As such, you need to include your accomplishments, especially for the past five years. This is not the time to worry about "bragging," as some candidates have said to me during career counseling. The resume also serves as the discussion jump-off point during your interview. This creates a question that may sound like this: "Tell me about your experience when you doubled the company's sales. Was that all a result of your efforts, or did other team members affect your results?"

When you began listing your most recent accomplishments in "What's Next? Here I Am," you were preparing to develop your resume. This was the reason I wanted you to list the most recent accomplishments and work backward.

If your accomplishments are not in your resume, they may not be discussed. Managers who have not been taught how to effectively interview may not know how to draw out accomplishments from you. If the accomplishment is on your resume, there is a better chance either the manager or you will bring it up during the interview.

Understanding that your resume is your marketing piece will possibly cause consternation among people who just discovered they are in a sales process. This is the time to get your creative (honest) juices flowing. If you are in marketing, you may go much further with a very creative presentation of your resume, possibly even on a DVD. But most positions require a more conventional approach.

So, you sweat all day writing the perfect resume. How much time will an experienced professional recruiter spend on it?

When I was on a recruitment consulting assignment with MCI, I hired a junior recruiter to assist me. The goal was to teach Andrea how to recruit. When I returned from each two-week interviewing trip, Andrea would bring a stack of resumes to my office to review before screening for our next trip. Because this was prior to e-mail and job boards, she generally brought me nearly 100 mailed or faxed resumes. One Monday, Andrea sat at a desk behind me while I read and separated the resumes into three stacks — definitely interested, definitely not interested and the (painful) take another look.

When I was finished, Andrea told me that she had timed me as I read all of those resumes. Since I was from the East Coast, my knee jerk response was, "Didn't you have enough work for today?" Andrea was the best person I ever hired. Sometimes she had the ESP of Radar O'Reilly from "M.A.S.H." She replied that because I was teaching her how to become a recruiter, she needed to know how much time to spend reading a resume. If she timed the attention I gave each resume, she would have a sense for the amount of time to spend. Then she asked me what grabbed my attention. I told her that I would tell her, but first I wanted to know what she discovered.

She informed me that I spent as little as two seconds on some resumes, and those went into the "definitely interested" and "definitely not interested" stacks. I spent as much as 12 seconds on other resumes. Those went into the "definitely not interested" and the "take another look" stacks. She said I averaged six seconds per resume.

You have two to 12 seconds to get the attention of a professional recruiter. What are we looking for?

Usually, when we are conducting searches, we know specifically what experience our clients require. In a very quick scan, we can determine if that experience is on the resume. As we scan for that experience, we are making mental notes on the impacts that person has made. If your resume was not tailored for that position, we are not mind readers, so your resume may go into the "wrong" stack.

The convention in resume writing is to write your resume in the third person, as if someone were writing about you, and drop the pronouns. You also write your resume in past tense, even the responsibilities you have in your current position.

Everyone who counsels candidates on resume writing has their own prejudices on the format. **These are the essentials: Keep it simple**

and easy to read. If you are successful here, you are more likely to attract the attention of a recruiter or hiring manager. After all, what do they typically look for in an "impact performer?" Excellent communication skills and the positive, measurable impacts you have made.

I have another important rule: **Keep your contact information in a plain, easy-to-read format. None of that fancy stuff like panels/boxes, bullet points/hyphens between addresses and phone numbers.** Also ensure that your contact information is in the body of the page, not the header. Why? Today most companies, including RecruiterGuy. com, store your resume in an applicant-tracking system. The optical character reading (OCR) software may not be able to understand the fancy stuff (or read your header) and your resume will go into the manual loading process. That means it may never get into the system. If it does not get into the system, no one will read it, you will never by interviewed and you will never know why.

Several times a year I receive resumes with no name or contact information. While I agree the information on your resume is important, being able to contact you should also be a priority. Your resume checklist needs to include a check to see if your name and contact information are easily found.

This an example of how your contact information may look:

> John Doe
> 1435 Main Street, Apt. A14
> Park City, UT 84060
> Home: (435) 555-0235 Work: (801) 555-1593
> jdoe@aol.com

There are essentially two kinds of resume document formats. Most people are familiar with the **chronological format** where you list your most recent experience and work back chronologically. The other format is the **functional format** where you group all of your accomplishments together and then simply list your most recent employers in backward order, including dates of employment.

The advantage of the **chronological format** is that recruiters and hiring managers have a better understanding of your responsibilities at each position and can see when you made impacts with employers. The potential disadvantage of the chronological resume is that short tenures stand out more, and if all of your true impacts are six years ago, managers wonder what you have been doing more recently.

The advantage of the **functional format** is the hope that recruiters and managers focus on your accomplishments and not on shorter tenures or the fact that accomplishments were made some time in your past. The disadvantage is that most professional recruiters know what to look for or ask when they see a functional resume. In my experience, the other major disadvantage is that many managers feel a candidate is trying to cover something up if they see a functional resume.

Which format is my preference? Based on my experience working with thousands of hiring managers over 29-plus years, I prefer the chronological resume. This way I can see what accomplishments were made — and when.

I like to see your name and contact information centered at the top of your resume (bold is nice). Look at the example above.

Then I like to see **Summary:** (bold) justified on the left margin. In your summary, list headlines of some of your important accomplishments — it would look something like this:

Summary: Saved company $150,000 by restructuring procurement process. Or, Consistently was 125 percent of quota in past five years.

You may add more details on your summary accomplishments in the body of your resume in the Professional Experience area.

If you graduated from college, **Education:** (bold) would be next, also justified on the left margin. List your most recent degree first. Then follow below with other degrees (if you earned them) in reverse order — most recent first. The reason that I prefer Education next is that many people in large companies who retrieve resumes have a checklist, and a college education many times is one of those checks. If Education is at the bottom of your resume, they may miss your impacts to get to

Education. One of the metrics they are measured on is the number of "qualified resumes" they forward to the corporate recruiter. If they are in a time crunch, your resume may not make the cut.

Here is a HUGE caution. Degrees are almost the easiest information to verify on a resume. If you did not get the last two PE credits, the college/university still requires you to earn them before you earn your degree. If you lie about your degree and are caught — and most likely today you will be caught — your offer will be rescinded or you will be fired. That's not something that you will want to discuss in your next interview.

Several years ago, a candidate that I introduced to a company showed a college degree from a major university. When I checked his credentials, I discovered that he attended the school but did not graduate. He was one class short of earning a degree. Over the years no one questioned his degree. Now we were interviewing him for a sales job for which he was eminently qualified (and that did not require a degree). When we discovered his deceit, I asked him why he lied about his degree. He responded that he thought he was "close enough." It cost him a job that he really wanted with a quality company.

This is a good time to talk briefly about honesty and resumes — and tell another story. There are two kinds of dishonesty and both have negative effects on your job search. The first is omitting skills that you enjoy doing and in which you have a great track record, sometimes known as impacts or accomplishments. This is a lie of omission. While there may be times that you want to leave off a degree earned, you never want to leave out impacts. You want to be prepared to discuss those impacts. If they are not on the resume, they may not be discussed.

The second type of dishonesty has many potentially negative impacts. This type of dishonesty is more important to discuss. It was alluded to in the paragraph about education. **Companies feel that resumes and applications are legal documents that represent your background, and as such, need to be truthful.** For instance, you may have had a job for a short time and for one or more reasons, it may not have worked out. Never let anyone suggest that you cover that job by stretching the end date of one job and the beginning date of the following job, effectively eliminating that experience from your resume.

A number of years ago, I was working with a candidate who was working in IT. This was an honest, hard-working person. I introduced him to a major corporation whose name would be familiar to you. They interviewed him and liked him so much that they extended him a contingent offer on the spot. The offer was contingent upon the successful completion of a background check and a drug test (both normal today).

He took the drug test and within a couple of days, the results came back and he passed. He turned in his resignation notice and was prepared to start at his new company in two weeks. On the Friday before his start on Monday, his offer was rescinded. He would not be allowed to start with the company. When I asked what happened, they told me that he covered up his employment at one firm by extending his end date at one company and start date at the next. When I called him, he said his resume writer suggested the change before I interviewed him — that way he would not have to discuss the short tenure.

The client told me they probably would have hired him anyway if they had known about the short tenure. Their feeling was that if he would "lie" about something as small as this, what would happen if they had a major issue? Great point! That is the basis of behavioral interviewing. The candidate was distraught because he lost the opportunity to work at a truly great company and he now had no job. His previous employer had already hired his replacement.

Employment applications typically have verbiage that states you could be fired at any time (even years later) if you misrepresent your experience.

Tell the truth on your resume.

Then write **Professional Experience:** (bold) justified on left column. Below Professional Experience, write the name of your current/last employer (bold/left justified) and your dates of employment (bold/right

justified). Below your employer's name, write your title (bold/left justified), followed by your most recent position. Then work backward.

This is an example of how that might look:

PROFESSIONAL EXPERIENCE:

IBM   **May 2007 to Present**

Director, Consulting Services

Responsible for the growth of this Washington, D.C., division of Government Services
Consulting. Managed 200 consultants in the government services arena. Grew the
division revenues by 65 percent in three years through hard work and client service.
Recruited key consultants for contracts with the Department of Agriculture and the
Department of Transportation.

- Secured contracts with government agencies where there was no previous
  contract with IBM.
- Grew the division profits 10 percent per year.
- Maintained high level of retention among consultants — 85 percent.

If you have worked with the same company for a long time and
held several positions within the company, write the name of your
employer (bold/left justified) and your total dates of employment
(bold/right justified). Skip a line and write your current/last title
(bold/left justified) and your dates in that position (bold/tab right).

This is an example of how that may look:

PROFESSIONAL EXPERIENCE:

IBM   **May 2003 to Present**

Director, Consulting Services   **August 2007 to Present**
Responsible for the growth of this Washington, D.C., division of Government Services Consulting. Managed 200 consultants in the government services arena. Grew the division revenues by 65 percent in 3 years through hard work and client service. Recruited key consultants for contracts with the Department of Agriculture and the Department of Transportation.

- Secured contracts with government agencies where there was no previous contract with IBM.
- Grew the division profits 10 percent per year.
- Maintained high level of retention among consultants — 85 percent.

Senior Manager, Consulting Services   **May 2003 to August 2007**
Managed 100 consultants working on a project for the Department of Agriculture. Responsible for client contact and client service. Negotiated a new contract to measure IT efficiencies within the Department of Agriculture's Animal and Plant Health Inspection Service.

- Grew profits for these projects by 40 percent over three years.

Understand that your information in the body describing responsibilities is not bold. When writing a resume, always begin sentences with action verbs in the past tense. Never begin a sentence with "Have developed." Begin the sentence "Developed." Write your resume with your responsibilities in paragraph format and accomplishments listed with bullet points. For some reason, some books recommend that you bullet point all of your activities. Based on my experience you should only list a few important accomplishments with bullet points for each position. Otherwise, in a resume with too many bullet points, your primary accomplishments may be overlooked. Remember, your resume is a marketing piece, so you want to focus on your accomplishments.

This is very important! **Do not put <u>any</u> personal information in your resume!** Like it or not, people use all of the information you give them to make a decision about whether you are a fit for their position or not. While companies cannot legally ask you for personal information, if you volunteer the information either on a resume or during an interview, they can use that information.

An example I have used in my talks is this. John Doe is an avionics engineer for Honeywell. He is interested in a position with Rockwell Collins in Cedar Rapids, Iowa. Jane Doe is an avionics engineer for Northrop Grumman and is interested in the same position at Rockwell Collins. When you look at their resumes, they have almost the same background in education and work experience.

John Doe goes sky diving a couple of times a year and listed that activity on his resume. Jane was advised not to list personal activities on her resume; therefore, she did not mention that she was the president of the sky diving club in Utah and goes out virtually every spring, summer and fall weekend to sky dive.

Both were called to interview with Rockwell Collins. The manager was surprised how close a call it was. Then she noticed that John Doe mentioned on his resume that he was a sky diver. She decided to hire Jane Doe because this was an important hire and she didn't want to lose a key employee to a sky-diving accident. It was only after Jane started that the manager heard that she was a true sky-diving enthusiast.

That is the reason you need to avoid including sky diving, mountain biking, whitewater rafting and other "dangerous" outside activities on your resume for professional positions. On the other hand, include them if you are applying for a position with an outfitter or a company that supplies that type of equipment. The recruiting and interviewing process is a discrimination process. The hiring manager is trying to determine who is the best qualified and the best fit. The hope is that the discrimination is legal. It's simply best to avoid putting any personal information on your resume.

You can add your work in associations or voluntary organizations, particularly if you were a leader. If you are interviewing in a manager's office and see a service club plaque, it is okay to ask about their relationship with that club. If you belong to the same club but a different chapter, you have formed the basis of a relationship.

Once you finish your resume, read it out loud word by word. Then read it again backward out loud. Then read it a third time forward out loud. Be aware that "form" and "from" both make it successfully through spell check. I see "manger" substituted for "manager" almost monthly. The same is true for "mange/manage," and their meanings are very different. There are many other words that match up that way — fan/fun/fin, chick/chuck, at/it, as/is, bite/kite, meet/meat, hear/here, etc. Use the "Find/Replace" function in your word processing program to check for these and other common words. Once you are totally satisfied it is perfect, ask someone who did not help you write your resume to edit it for you. **Remember spell check? One candidate wrote in a cover letter that they were a "detale oriented professional" (does that hurt?) — Maybe not so detail oriented!**

Only then is it almost safe to give to a company — just read it aloud one more time. Remember, your resume is your representation of you. If it is written carelessly, that is a reflection of your work.

In the spring of 1994, I was asked to present the recruitment process to 16 visiting Russian businesspeople. They were from the oil companies in southern Russia. Prior to the Soviet Union split, there was a central bureau that matched candidates with companies. Candidates had no interviews, no tour, no decision. When they told you to report to that company, that's where you worked. The companies were on the other side of the coin. There was no interviewing process. They took the person the central bureau sent. They did not need to attract candidates. There were no recruiters. They picked up the phone and called the bureau — and people reported on Monday.

After the Soviet Union had split, there was no central employment bureau that would match candidates with companies. After the split, those companies now needed to learn how to compete for candidates and how to select the best candidates. That's why they were in northern Virginia that day. I do not speak Russian and I suspect most of them did not speak English, so I had a translator.

When we discussed resumes, I told the businesspeople that a resume should be the perfect reflection of a candidate's work. If there is a typo in their resume, I… (with that I scrunched up a piece of paper and used a hook shot to toss it into the trash can). It was fun to watch their eyes follow the ball of paper, then glance back quickly at the translator who translated what I said. Then they laughed.

Your resume is the representation of your best work when you are trying to make the most important sale of your life — your ability to make impacts with a new company.

Another candidate wrote in a cover letter that he "would be a good fit for MCI" (my client). Then he wrote that companies such as Boeing (instead of MCI) need professionals who understood marketing — and then proceeded to use two more company names in place of MCI. I can't imagine that he was successful attracting an interview with that letter!

When you write a resume, it is best to understand that it is really a base for future resumes. Before you apply to a company, it is important to change words in your resume to reflect the company's job description. For instance, perhaps in your resume you were called a buyer at your last company. When you read the job description, it was almost a perfect match for your "buyer" position but their title is "purchasing agent." Then they used "purchased" instead of "bought." Save your base resume with the name of the company and date. Then make the changes to reflect the same work and different descriptive verbs, nouns and adjectives.

Why go through this effort? Recruiters tend to take keywords from their job descriptions to search the resume database in their applicant tracking system (ATS). If they choose "purchased" as one of their key words and you wrote "bought," chances are pretty good that your resume will not be selected; therefore, it is best to make those changes before forwarding your resume.

Think of the applicant tracking system as a Labrador Retriever. When the recruiter types in a few keywords, it is like showing the rawhide bone to the dog. Then they click "search" in the ATS. The computer gets all excited just like a dog, and when it returns in a couple of seconds (not like the dog...), it shows its excitement by saying in the results that it is 90 percent sure this person is a good match. Its determination that a candidate is a good match comes from seeing the search words (keywords) multiple times in your resume.

Therefore, if you are replying to an Internet posting, it is good to have another copy of your resume that is saved under that company's name and keywords. At the bottom of that resume, type "Keywords:" and then list all potential keywords from their job description where you have that experience. It will help raise the confidence of the ATS that you have the best experience. This is one of the reasons applicant-tracking systems will not replace humans in the search process.

Remember to put your name on each page of your resume. Because your name is on the first page, the best practice is to use the header for the following pages — page numbers justified left and your name justified on the right. It is almost normal for resume pages to separate on a manager's desk. Many times I have watched managers shuffle papers on their desk to find the second or third page of a candidate's resume. Soon they will simply use their monitor or electronic pad.

This a sample chronological resume:

John Doe
1435 Main Street, Apt. A14
Park City, UT 84060
Home: (435) 555-0235 Work: (801) 555-1593
jdoe@aol.com

SUMMARY: Grew division revenues 65 percent over three years... Grew division profits incrementally... Secured new government contracts for IBM... Maintained 85 percent consultant retention rate.

EDUCATION: MBA, University of Iowa 1998

BS, Business, University of Utah

PROFESSIONAL EXPERIENCE:

IBM   **May 2004 to Present**

Director, Consulting Services   **August 2007 to Present**

Responsible for the growth of this Washington, D.C., division of Government Services Consulting. Managed 200 consultants in the government services arena. Grew the division revenues by 65 percent in three years through hard work and client service. Recruited key consultants for contracts with the Department of Agriculture and the Department of Transportation.

Secured contracts with government agencies where there was no previous contract with IBM.

Grew the division profits 10 percent per year.

Maintained high level of retention among consultants – 85 percent.

Senior Manager, Consulting Services   **May 2004 to August 2007**

Managed 100 consultants working on a project for the Department of Agriculture. Responsible for client contact and client service. Negotiated a new contract to measure IT efficiencies within the Department of Agriculture's Animal and Plant Health Inspection Service.

Grew profits for these projects by 40 percent over three years.

Booz, Allen, Hamilton   **May 1998 to April 2004**

Consultant

Project Manager for government process improvement projects. Created the first template for a financial process improvement project at Commerce Department. Developed spreadsheets that highlighted waste.

Led a team responsible for the Census Bureau financial restructuring, saving taxpayers $50 million in the first year.

ASSOCIATIONS: Lean Enterprise Institute, presented at conference "Instituting Lean Process Improvement in Federal Agencies."

This is a sample functional resume:

John Doe
1435 Main Street, Apt. A14
Park City, UT 84060
Home: (435) 555-0235 Work: (801) 555-1593
jdoe@aol.com

SUMMARY: Grew division revenues 65 percent over three years… Grew division profits incrementally… Secured new government contracts for IBM… Maintained 85 percent consultant retention rate.

EDUCATION: MBA, University of Iowa 1998
BS, Business, University of Utah

SKILLS: Excellent Manager, Creative, Experienced Kaizen Event Leader, Budget-Oriented Leader.

IMPACTS: Led a team responsible for the Census Bureau financial restructuring, saving taxpayers $50 million in the first year.

Grew the division revenues by 65 percent in three years through hard work and client service.

Grew profits for these projects by 40 percent over three years.

Secured contracts with government agencies where there was no previous contract with IBM.

Grew the division profits 10 percent per year.

Maintained high level of retention among consultants – 85 percent.

ASSOCIATIONS: Lean Enterprise Institute, presented at conference "Instituting Lean Process Improvement in Federal Agencies"

EXPERIENCE:

IBM	Director, Consulting Services	May 2004 to Present
Booz, Allen, Hamilton	Consultant	May 1998 to April 2004

While obviously both resumes were created for these examples, you can see why experienced hiring managers like to see when impacts were made.

Every company has its own culture and focus. In your research on your prospective employers, go to every page on their web site to get a sense for them and their priorities. If they have community service pages, read them because it will give you a sense for their social responsibility. More important, you may volunteer at one or more of the charities they sponsor. Those would obviously need to be on your resume.

Developing an effective resume is important for creating an interesting interview. The candidates who have interesting interviews are the ones who generally receive offers.

Take time now to create your resume. Remember, this is a process. To be successful, let's lay a good foundation and then move forward.

What is the role of cover letters? Actually, most recruiters who have been in the business for a long time do not read cover letters. Unless I am trying to get a sense for a candidate's writing style, I do not read the cover letter. There is no guarantee they even wrote the cover letter. Many resume writers or career counselors either write the resume and letter or counsel the person what and how to convey the information. If a cover letter is required by the company, compose one that is succinct. Cover the information required and request an interview.

This chapter is so important that we have two checklists — the Resume Checklist and the Job-Search Process Checklist.

RESUME CHECKLIST

❑ Is the information on your resume accurate? Honesty is the only policy.

❑ Is your name and contact information easily found?

❑ Are your degree and graduation date accurate?

❏ Did you write your resume in third person, past tense?

❏ Did you drop the pronouns and begin your sentences with action verbs?

❏ Did you discuss your most-recent experience first followed chronologically by previous experience?

❏ Did you include all of your measurable impacts in your resume?

❏ Have you read your resume aloud? Did you run spell check? Did you run "Find/Replace" for words like *mange, manger, from* and *form*?

❏ Has a friend or associate read your resume as an editor? Did they look at spelling and grammar?

❏ Have you saved your resume in your word processing software? Did you print it — just in case?

❏ If a cover letter is required, have you composed one that is succinct and covers all of the information required by the company?

After you have completed this checklist, let's move to your job-search checklist. Think of RecruiterGuy as your search project manager as he sits on your shoulder.

JOB-SEARCH PROCESS CHECKLIST

Put a check mark next to the completed items on your list. Work to complete the ones that are not finished. This process will help you find your next job. Your job now is to complete each task.

❏ Review your list of professional and personal skills to see if you can improve the descriptive impact verbs. Only use words that you use in normal conversation. It's really embarrassing to use the wrong verb.

❏ Review the examples of the situations that required your skills. After thinking about your examples over the last few days, are there better examples that you can use? Again, the format is to discuss what you did as a result of the situation. Then discuss what happened as a result of your influence or direct action for each skill or attribute that demonstrates your skill. People remember stories, not lists.

❏ Develop a list of your positive, measurable impacts over the past 10 years, with focus on the last five years. List them from the most recent impacts backward. Develop a situation, action and result around each impact — and what you learned. If you still have old annual reviews, read through them for impacts that you may have forgotten.

❏ Review and add to your list of 250 names of family, friends and acquaintances, neighbors, former peers/managers in your last company and previous companies, high school and college alumni, pastor/rabbi/spiritual mentor, banker, attorney, real estate agents, professors, doctors and acquaintances from the health club. Look up their contact information in your address book, the phonebook or use Google or Bing to search for them on the Internet.

❏ Join LinkedIn and invite everyone you feel can help you — and who you can help somewhere. Remember, it is important to give. When people accept your invitation, go through their network and see if there may be contacts you forgot to enter on your list. This action may help you remember additional people to add to your spreadsheet. Remember, people know other people — and LinkedIn is a great example of how it can work.

❏ You have developed your "Here I Am!" speech. Continue to practice it with people you know well first. It can be as simple as, "Hey, I am working on a differentiator for my candidacy. Would you mind listening to it as I practice?" Most people would love to help you.

Now you are developing your brand as a candidate. Your resume is now completed. The combination of resume, LinkedIn profile, and "Here I Am!" speech are your primary marketing preparations for networking and then interviewing.

If you have not completed all of these steps, put your bookmark back in here and finish these processes. Remember, these are the fundamentals that will help you find your next job. Skating through these processes only extends your job-search process.

Let's pause here for a second. As you have been preparing your search, have you considered starting your own business? If you have, many community colleges bring businesspeople in to conduct classes on starting a business. Additionally, you should contact the Small Business Administration to discuss the process. You may want to explore this avenue to utilize the skills that you enjoy using.

Our next process is one of the most enjoyable if you try to give back to other people. You will learn about them and their dreams, and possibly contribute to their success. Meanwhile, some of them may be instrumental in helping you succeed in your search. This is the Effective Networking Process!

CHAPTER 4
EFFECTIVE NETWORKING TO
YOUR NEXT POSITION!

Are you tired of posting to the black holes on the Internet? You know them — tantalizing job titles and job postings where no one ever answers other than the automated thank you response.

Stand up and take control of your search! All too often, candidates try the easy route to find a job — simply getting on the Internet and posting their resume to dozens of companies at a time. Unfortunately, after all of those postings, they never receive a call.

Then frustration sets in and you find yourself complaining that it's all a waste of time — and then you do it again tomorrow and the next day.

Please understand that Internet job postings are essentially automated newspaper ads. The beauty of the Internet from a company perspective is that instead of having to handle each resume that is mailed or faxed in, the Internet response never needs to be handled by a human. That line should give you something to think about. Now you know why you never receive a call.

Some companies out there are excellent recruiting machines. But in my experience, most companies are trying to recruit the same way they always have, without really learning that recruiting is sales. They do not understand that the candidate experience is as important as the consumer experience, if not more important. Chances are, most companies that do not understand the importance of the candidate experience are the same companies you have not heard from. Isn't it amazing that sometimes you do not hear from companies even after you told them in your inquiry that you are a happy client?

Recruiting is sales!

I understand that you are tired of hearing about networking, and how many jobs are filled by networking and networking breakfasts and networking on social media and networking on the phone and networking this and networking that. No one seems to want to slow down and truly describe networking. Everyone seems to be too busy networking to explain it.

The short answer is that networking can occur in every conversation that you have. It is simply the exchange of ideas that can benefit one or both parties. Networking is not only used in job searches, it is successfully utilized in business development at all levels. It's not some huge monster.

Networking is just one conversation in person or over the phone at a time. It's the consistent use of those interactions that benefit people. Now that you have a better sense of networking, it should become easier. Of course, those first few conversations may be tough to begin. Once you start seeing some results from your networking, you will build confidence in your ability to contribute to these conversations. You may never be a great fan of the networking process, but you will become more confident in your skills at working the process.

One very important concept of networking is that successful networking involves both give and take. The first step in successful networking is listening. Focus on the person who is talking with you. Ask yourself, "How can I help them?" Ask them questions to clarify your thinking. Then try to make helpful suggestions for them.

While looking for a job, it is easy to be focused on your situation without thinking about the other person. After all, you do have bills to pay. Your cost to belong to the networking society is your ability to give back to the people you contact. Once you demonstrate that you will give suggestions to the other people with whom you network, they will take your call more enthusiastically and offer corresponding suggestions to you.

The law of nature is, "What you give is what you will receive." Be a giving person during this process. Be an active listener, a person who assimilates information and then creates a thoughtful response. Pay attention in every conversation. You never know when a small clue of an opportunity may emerge.

Be careful that you are not like a singer warming up — me, me, me, me!

What is the most effective way to network for a new position?

The first step is to develop your "Here I Am!" speech. This is also known as an elevator speech or one-minute commercial. It needs to come from your heart and give a quick snapshot of your background, your current situation and what you want to do next. It shouldn't be longer than 30 seconds. You worked on your "Here I Am!" speech in Chapter 2, "What's Next? Here I Am!" I gave an example of an effective "Here I Am!" speech.

Once you are comfortable with what you will tell contacts, it is important to develop a list of people to contact. I discussed this list creation in depth in Chapters 1 and 2. Don't limit that list to those who know you well. Include any people who know who you are. Your list could include people from your former employer who know your work ethic (this could be a double-edged sword), friends, neighbors, people from church, a store or your bank. How about the parents of your children's friends? Include everyone. The more the better. During a job search, your most important commodity is names and phone numbers, particularly referred names and phone numbers. Develop a spreadsheet of everyone you know, including all acquaintances, with a phone number and information about where they work (if you know). Do you belong to a service organization like Rotary Club or Lion's Club? Do you belong to Toastmasters? This may be a good time to join some of those organizations. Remember, networking involves giving back to your community.

Develop a second spreadsheet of companies that you have targeted. Once you have identified potential target companies, spend some time researching them. Comb through their web site. Where are the opportunities for you to help them? Try to understand their challenges. Who is their competition? Based on their web site, what challenges can you help them overcome? This information is important while networking and during an interview. During research, take copious notes — either cut and paste your notes on the company to a word processor document or print pages of its web site. You know how you learn best. During your research, you may discover the company is not a good fit for you. That's fine. It is as important for you to cross companies off your list as add them. Their competition may be the right company.

Knowledge is power!

When my daughter was looking at colleges, we spent a couple of days traveling and visiting several colleges and looking for the right fit for her. As we were driving home, she apologized that none of those colleges seemed like the right one. I told her not to apologize. "We now know three colleges are not a fit. Let's keep looking." Eventually, she walked onto a college campus and said, "This is the one!" It turned out to be a great fit for her, both personally and educationally.

You are going through the same process right now. Some companies are added to your list. Others are crossed off. That is part of the process. Remember, you are trying to find that job that is so much fun you'll say, "Wow! I even get paid to do this!"

Finally, if you have a LinkedIn network, identify people you want to contact there; some of these are your "cold calls." Use the LinkedIn network to meet people who may be instrumental to setting up an interview with you. We worked on developing your list over the last few chapters. Your list gives you a track to run. This is how important networking is to your success, because you do want to run through the finish line to a successful new job, correct?

In a serious job search, you need to faithfully call at least four new contacts per day for three months. If you do, the law of averages will work in your favor and you will most likely receive interviews and an acceptable offer. Now you know why names and their phone numbers are your most important commodities. Do the math. If you do not faithfully call those numbers of people, it will take you longer to find a job — unless you are very lucky.

Now it is time to clarify one small and very important piece of information. Note that I said call, not e-mail. Companies are doing much better protecting their networks from outside attacks and spam e-mails. Your contact may not receive your e-mail. On the other hand, they may see that you sent an e-mail but are so busy they didn't have time to respond immediately — and it was buried in their mass of e-mail. I have been that person. Wasn't hell paved with good intentions?

When you call your first contacts, tell them the reason for your call (networking) and ask if you can take a minute to tell them about your background. Now give them your "Here I Am!" speech. Then ask them whom they recommend that you talk with next. I guarantee that if you just ask them if they have an opening at their company, their kneejerk response 98 percent of the time will be "No." Try to get at least four or five people's names and numbers from each person you call. These are your warm referrals. They may say they don't know anyone. Then ask, "Whom do you know at ABC company?" or, "Do you know anyone who lives in New England (or any-where)?" Asking the latter question may help you get to a different part of the country without knowing anyone there yourself. **Remember six degrees of separation — by conducting six directed conversations, you may reach anyone in the United States.**

What is a "warm referral?" When someone calls you and says that a friend or business acquaintance gave them your name and number, you are more open to receiving the call, right? Not only that, you do not want to disappoint your friend so you try to help that caller. That's why you seek warm referrals. A person you call out of the blue may not even take your call. If they do take your call, they may not be as likely to help you. (You still should make cold calls because they can lead to more warm referrals!)

Many times someone I respected asked me to meet with a person who was out of work. I set aside some time and met with them. Why? I wanted to maintain the respect of my contact and meet or exceed their expectations. Remember to give back when you have the opportunity.

When insurance companies hire young salespeople, they train them to call family and friends first. Why? Those typically are the least threatening calls. That's also why you should practice your new networking skills with friends and family. They will be happy to give you pointers, especially brothers and sisters...

All kidding aside, make your easy calls first and then work toward the more difficult cold calls. Most people will be willing to help you. Occasionally, someone may be having a bad day and act like a jerk. Understand that you may have been the 40th networking call they received that day, and they were nice to the first 38 people. If it makes you feel any better, hang up after saying good-bye, wait a couple of seconds, then pick up the phone and listen for the dial tone. If you hear the dial tone — and only if you hear the dial tone — you may say "Jerk!" If you don't hear the dial tone, and still say "Jerk!" you may make my next book!

So we have discussed many elements of networking but haven't discussed networking meetings. They are another way for you to meet people. As one of the organizers of the Park City Career Network, I can say we encourage members to help each other.

There are many other organizations that promote networking among the members. Your local chamber of commerce may offer "After Hours" meetings. Chamber members are generally given free admission and members of the community may join the "After Hours" for a small admission price. In my experience at these meetings, there are cliques and few people really interested in true networking. But people are only as interested in you as you are in them. You have the time. Use it to meet new people. Imagine the little RecruiterGuy on your shoulder encouraging you to meet just one more person.

Several years ago I attended a conference. One of the presentations was by a noted author who presented on networking. During his presentation, he mentioned that when you are participating in networking meetings, totally focus on the person with whom you are chatting. Obviously, if you are looking around the room while chatting with them, they know you really are not interested in their conversation.

After the presentation, I went up to thank him for his information. Ironically, as we were chatting, he was looking around the room.

Treat people with respect. If you can make suggestions to help them, do so. If not, nicely excuse yourself and either leave or meet someone else. While "working a room," work really hard to maintain eye contact with the one person or group of people in your conversation. Do not look for your next conversation. Remember to pay attention. Sometimes a person will say something that triggers the right question from you and leads you somewhere totally unexpected — and worthwhile.

What else important could happen after you give your "Here I Am!" speech? They could ask you, "Are you interviewing with us?" Ahh, music to my ears! That's the response you may seek. If you are not interviewing with them, ask them who to contact within their firm or if they would be willing to introduce you. This is how you network your way into a job.

We've discussed some of the mechanics of networking. Now let's discuss the nature of networking and use some stories to illustrate it.

Networking can happen unexpectedly. It does not have to be scheduled, but you have to be prepared to switch it on immediately. When you are out there meeting people, you can have the opportunity to meet other new people.

In the 1980s when I was a contingent (fee-based) recruiter in Washington, D.C., one of my very good clients was *The Washington Post's* IT group. In those days, *The Washington Post* had an excellent IT department, one of the best in the area. We had a great relationship. They knew that my referrals were right on target.

One day I was downtown, not far from The Post building, meeting with another client. After the meeting, I stopped at a nearby restaurant for lunch. After I was seated, I began to let my mind and ears wander. Eventually, a conversation at the next table caught my attention. Obviously, the woman was an IT professional (in those days we called them data processing), and she was being interviewed by a recruiter. As their conversation proceeded, I decided that she would be a great fit for *The Post*. She had the perfect experience and attitude to succeed there. Since Katharine Graham was the publisher at *The Post*, there was no glass ceiling.

I decided that I was going to meet that candidate. Fortunately for me, my vigilance was rewarded. The other recruiter got up from the table, leaving her sitting there by herself.

Given the opportunity, I leaned over, apologized for listening in on her conversation, and asked if she would be interested in working for *The Washington Post*. She said, "Sure!" I asked her if she had an additional resume. She replied "No."

Then I asked her if she was available to interview the next morning at *The Post*. She replied that she was. I told her to fax her resume to me (no e-mail in those days) and to expect an interview at *The Post* at 9 the next morning. She agreed.

When she faxed her resume to me, I forwarded it to the manager at *The Post*. He called me back right away. I asked if the team was available to interview her the next morning. He said that he liked her background and would set everything up. When I called her back to set up the interview, I was so confident that she would receive an offer, I told her to expect an offer by 11 a.m. (Today, I may not be so over-confident!)

At 10:30 the next morning, the manager called me and was laughing. He said that he was going to extend her an offer. He had a problem — all three managers who interviewed her wanted her on their teams — and another manager was interviewing her right then. They were going to have to decide which team she would join.

The candidate called me about 11:15, right after leaving *The Post*. She was also laughing. She said her last interview was over at 10:50. The manager met with her and just before 11 a.m., he extended her an offer and she accepted. She asked how I knew. I replied that I knew my client that well.

A postscript to that story is that the other recruiter obviously found out that she accepted the job at *The Post* a couple of weeks later. He was very upset when she told him how we met, even wanted me to pay for lunch! He probably never left a candidate alone in a restaurant again after our incident. Neither did I!

Bottom line — prospects for networking surround you and you never know when one will strike up a conversation with you. Be prepared to accept that conversation.

Let's talk about social networking. During the past couple of years, you have been bombarded with all kinds of social-networking opportunities — MySpace, LinkedIn, Facebook, Twitter, YouTube, Plaxo, etc. And more are on the way. If you are not comfortable with iPhones, Palm Pre, Android and other handheld computers that allow you to talk, check e-mail, and set appointments simultaneously, you probably are not very comfortable with the social-media tools. On the other hand, maybe you're more like, "OMG U text 4 hrs!" and know these tools are simply arrows in your quiver.

Separate your social networking from your professional networking. If you connect with a company on Facebook, it can see your posts and pictures. Some may be embarrassing, or worse, disqualify you from a job.

The owner of a recruiting firm told me they had introduced a candidate to a financial institution. The interview went very well, so well they extended a contingent offer to the candidate. The candidate accepted their offer. The company is very thorough when they vet their candidates. The client looked up the candidate on Facebook. The person enabled everyone to see his pages. Evidently some of his posts to friends were viewed to be unacceptable for this firm and they rescinded the offer. Remember, everything that is public may be viewed and used in the final decision to determine if you are the best fit for a position. Like it or not, you are constantly being measured by someone.

Professionally, the current standard for social-media networking is LinkedIn.com. More than 60 million people worldwide have profiles on LinkedIn. Once you begin developing your brand as a candidate or employee, it is good to develop your profile on LinkedIn. Working on LinkedIn may take as much time as you want to spend. That is my caution to candidates and companies alike: Every networking/

sourcing method costs something. Sometimes it is money and sometimes it is time. If it is time, it must be done well or you (or they) lose credibility with the audience.

Recruiters recognized early how powerful LinkedIn could be as a recruiting tool. What's better than a free list of names with their professional backgrounds? Everything is to like here. From a candidate's perspective, it also is a potentially strong networking tool because it can be a great way to introduce yourself to a company you like or to a new region where you want to move.

As you complete your profile, keep in mind that recruiters search for key words. They may be words that are in their job descriptions or they may simply be titles. In some industries/companies you may be a "buyer." In others your title may be "purchasing agent." Ensure that both are in your profile. You may be a sales professional, account manager, account executive or two dozen other titles. What do you do? You sell something to someone.

Your LinkedIn summary gives you an opportunity to discuss your brand and impacts over the past several years. If you have presented to groups and want to continue doing so, be sure to list at least some of your recent presentations. The information in your summary should give readers a sense of your proficiencies.

If you are someone who reads literature that applies to your industry, add the application that gives you the opportunity to review books. Talk about your experience and how that book may affect others in the same area or industry. All of the positive information you add to your LinkedIn profile gives other people a sense for who you are.

If you have a presentation that you feel would be valuable to share, you may use a Google application to add it to your profile. This is another way to demonstrate your knowledge within your field and develop the perception of expertise. People's perception is their reality.

After I presented the webinar "Why the Best Qualified Candidate Rarely Gets the Job," I added the presentation to my LinkedIn profile and have received thanks and congratulations for the presentation. This is a way for me to provide potential clients a reason to have a conversation with me.

Remember that networking is a two-way street. Part of your cost of participation is to benefit the other people in your network. As you link with other people and grow your network, some people may have really impressed you with their actions when you worked with them. Write a sincere recommendation for them on LinkedIn that describes a situation or position where they were particularly effective, and mention the positive impacts of their actions. By the way, write the recommendation in a word-processing program to take advantage of spell check and double check to ensure you spelled their name correctly. They may decide to accept your recommendation. Some of those people will write a recommendation for you, but don't request it from them. The recommendations that you receive will be shared for others to view on your profile page.

At the top of your profile, there is a menu that goes across the top of your page. Click on "Groups," and then on "Groups Directory." Search the groups to see which ones apply to the area that you are searching, and then apply to become a member of the appropriate groups. Generally, most groups accept new members as long as there is some type of connection to them. Most of those groups post jobs within the group, so this is an excellent opportunity to see what other members are working on. Additionally, members may ask public questions looking for responses from other members. This is an additional way for you to build on your brand and show that you are an expert in a particular area.

As you drop down the right column on your "home" page on your LinkedIn profile, LinkedIn uses a fuzzy logic to suggest people that you may want to connect with on LinkedIn. All you need to do is click on a name and invite the person to join your LinkedIn network (Click on "add to your network"). I prefer to write my own succinct invitation instead of the stock invitation provided by LinkedIn. **A personal request to link is more likely to be accepted than a stock invitation.**

As you are creating your LinkedIn profile, people will begin to discover you and ask you to join their LinkedIn network. Welcome the invitations that make sense. LinkedIn coaches you only to accept or invite the people you know well; however, I accept other people that appear to have legitimate, appropriate job histories that match my interests. I do not accept everyone.

Further down the right column, you see how many people have looked at your profile in the past day or so. Don't get upset over those numbers. You are reaching out, not driving people to you.

Finally, on the right column you see "Answers." You may edit the area of questions that you receive by clicking "edit." Once you save that area, you may begin to respond to questions within that area of expertise. The recipient of your response may select that you had either a good answer or a best answer. When you have accumulated 30 best answers, LinkedIn gives you an "expert" title in that area of expertise. Obviously, responding to the questions in a positive, helpful manner may attract companies to you.

On the other hand, beware of your posts. Never post something that you would not want to read on the front page of the *New York Times* tomorrow. LinkedIn can provide you with a wonderful opportunity to blast someone or some company. Don't do it! You can understand how poorly that reflects on you as an expert in your field.

For instance, I responded to a question on whether age discrimination exists. It was interesting to read the posts of unemployed human resource folks; some of these definitely were not professional. My attitude has always been that if a company is silly enough to discriminate against me on the basis of age, I really would not want to work with them. A couple of people commenting on the topic were just being a little too forthcoming about their feelings. I wrote them a personal note and asked them if they were the one looking for a human resource professional and saw their response, would they contact someone with that response? The next day both posts were removed.

Beware of the time you spend in social media. Social media can be very seductive. Always shoot for balance while networking. Your most productive time needs to be spent on the phone or in person.

While I was a young recruiter, a friend always referred to the prime candidate contact time as "Prime Time." Use Prime Time to do your phone and personal networking. Set aside social media for your non-Prime Time work, such as early mornings or evenings.

As you develop your network, it is good to ask the people with whom you are networking what information you may be able to give them. I always try to contribute ideas and suggestions when I have a conversation with anyone. It's good to ask, "Have you tried...?" Another good question is "What has been your biggest obstacle so far?"

So far, we have not discussed the role of professional recruiters. You may expect a person who has been successful in that role since 1981 to trumpet the services of professional recruiting firms. Professional recruiters do play an important role in a job-search process; however, it is easier for a recruiter to earn a fee when a candidate is working than when he is out of work. Companies feel they can find people who are looking actively for jobs without paying a fee.

Therefore, it is best to develop a relationship with a professional recruiter while you are happily employed. Accept their calls warmly. If it seems they are calling too often, simply ask them to spread out the time between calls. Time is money to recruiters and they should accept your request gracefully. If they do find an interesting opportunity, feel free to explore it. If it is the right opportunity for you, you may find yourself in an exciting new position.

Many times, I have developed professional relationships with candidates without being aware of any positions that would interest them at the time. I just wanted to get to know them, their interests, their skills and person-ality. We would talk as they made impacts in their current position. We often discussed their excitement about something that went very well and the frustra-tion when things weren't going well. A number of times, a year or two passed before the perfect position became available. When I called them, we already had a relationship and the process proceeded smoothly to their next position. Rarely does this process happen quickly, but the example at *The Post* above demonstrates how unexpectedly quickly it can happen.

Also understand a professional recruiter's responsibility is to the client. Clients pay recruiters to find the best possible match for them. They are not paid by the candidate. I wish I had a dollar for every time I've heard from a candidate that one recruiter or another "didn't do anything for me." Usually, I nicely say that it's not the recruiter's job to do something for them, but one will probably be happy to make some suggestions for their search.

It is important to notify everyone who helped you when you are successful finding your next job. Then ask them if there was any information that you may be able to give them as a result of your networking.

A number of years ago in Cedar Rapids, Iowa, a young woman called me and asked if I could spend some time with her to discuss her job search. She had recently graduated from college and I had known her since her soccer playing days in high school. I invited her to lunch at a restaurant where we could talk. We spent two hours discussing the job-search process and how to network her way to her first job. After lunch, she offered to pay for lunch. I told her that she could buy me a lunch after she started her first job.

After a few weeks, I received a call. She was excited to inform me that she had just accepted a job. She said, "Now I can buy you lunch!" A couple of weeks after her first check, we went to lunch. She was excited to tell me that my suggestions helped her. Why did her story make this book? She was one of the very few people who took my time and then got back to thank me for my time.

People in your network remember when you thank them — and when you don't. Think about the potential future impact.

Another potential source of networking is career fairs. I know some candidates refer to them as "cattle calls" and other not-so-nice names. But a career fair is a great place to meet people who work for companies that you may target, and to help you identify others that you did not know were in the area. I have spoken at more than 50 career fairs nationwide and worked a couple of hundred career fairs representing clients.

A skilled candidate may work a career fair as well as a teenager working Walt Disney World! Before the day of the career fair, look to see which employers plan to attend. Then go to their web site to check their open positions and any interesting press releases. They may not have open positions posted, but they may have announced an expansion — the job postings just haven't appeared yet. The fair organizers will usually post a map showing where the different companies will be located. Understand that they don't always show up where they are supposed to, but generally they will be where you expect.

On the day of the career fair, print 10 more resumes than you expect to need. Do not fold your resumes. Bring them in a portfolio where you can also take notes.

When you arrive at a career fair, they usually will ask you to register prior to entering. Sometimes they allow you to register electronically and use a memory stick to load your resume into their system. Many times they forward all resumes to the companies that participate in the fair.

Now, I am going to give you the secret to working a career fair. It is one that every teenager knows when "working" an amusement park or a ski resort. People are wonderfully consistent. Typically, they stop at the first booth that interests them. They may even stand in a line there. Meanwhile, the people manning the booths in the back are lonely. So unless a company that interests you in front has no candidates, go directly to companies that interest you in the back of the hall. Depending on the size of the hall and the number of companies, you have about 10 minutes before other people join you. These 10 minutes can be very valuable because everyone is fresh. Later in the day, the recruiters who would rather be anywhere else may ignore you — pretty strange, huh? I've seen them pull up stakes a couple of hours early. Usually, that's when I meet the most interesting candidates because they were working earlier!

As you work a career fair, it is easy to tell which companies are experienced in dealing with candidates at one. It also gives you a sense for the company. For instance, prior to a career fair when I am representing my clients, I walk through the hall just prior to the opening of the doors. As RecruiterGuy, I want to know who my true competition is for good candidates. Typically, they have arranged their booths to be welcoming to candidates. Other companies keep their tables between them and the candidates. That is commonly referred to as a barrier. Many times how the booth is set also is a good indication of their culture. Are they open or are they closed? Are they welcoming or not?

Generally, I try to attract one or more of my clients' managers to the fair to work with me. It is a great opportunity for them to see some of the quality of available candidates in the community and possibly even interview one or two of them. When a sharp candidate approaches, I bring them inside the booth, listen to their "Here I Am!" speech, look at their resume and then make a quick decision how to proceed. If they are a potential candidate for the manager who is with me, I excuse myself from the candidate for a minute to speak with the manager. The manager will look at the resume. If we agree to proceed, I suggest that the manager take the candidate to a nearby restaurant to interview. The manager is happy for an excuse to leave the booth, and the candidate is excited to have an interview so quickly. It's a win-win! More than one person has been hired that way.

Remember to pay attention as you work the career fair.

In 1996, I was working with a De La Rue subsidiary in Iowa. My tablecloth had De La Rue and the logo on both the front and on top of the table. I was in Des

Moines, meeting candidates at the career fair that day. Toward the end of the day when things were slowing down and there were no candidates in front of me, a sharply dressed young man was walking past me. I stepped out and asked him what he was looking for. He said, "You probably don't have what I'm looking for." I asked again what he sought. He said, "Positions in Europe." I asked him why he was walking past a company named De La Rue. I forwarded his resume to corporate headquarters in the UK.

The primary tools of networking are your list, your "Here I Am!" speech and your perseverance. There is one more very important attribute that comes into play while networking: a positive mental attitude. People do what you expect them to do; therefore, if you expect them to blow you off, your self-fulfilling expectation will cause you to say something that causes them to blow you off. Always make calls with a smile on your face and the expectation of success. It will greatly improve your success rate.

Now you are moving forward on your search. You are beginning to gain some success and momentum! Can interviews be far behind? You have graduated from the early items of your checklist. They are now your responsibility.

JOB-SEARCH PROCESS CHECKLIST —
Preparing for Your Interviews

❑ Review the examples of the situations that required your skills. After thinking about your examples over the last few days, are there better examples that you can use? As you are doing your research on companies, new examples will continue to flow into your mind if you allow them. Again, the format is to discuss the situation and what you did as a result of the situation. Then discuss what happened as a result of your influence or direct action for each skill or attribute that demonstrates your skill. People remember stories, not lists. These stories are important to relate during your interviews.

❑ Develop a list of your positive, measurable impacts over the past 10 years, with focus on the last five years. List them from the most recent impacts backward. Develop a situation, action and result around each impact — and what you learned. If you still have old annual reviews, read through them for impacts that you may have forgotten. Both of these tasks prepare you for impressive interviewing!

❑ As you network, faithfully add new names to your spreadsheet and note how they may be related to other connections.

❑ You have developed your resume, "Here I Am!" speech and brand as a candidate.

❑ You have begun talking with people (networking). **Track your results. Remember, you are in a sales process. Working in a sales process, it is important to know your numbers.** While networking, it is important to track how many calls (phone and personal) you make per day. Then track the results of each call (Think baseball statistics — track measurable activity). To maintain a positive mental attitude, it is important to know your averages.

For instance, it is important to know that for every three calls you make, you have one conversation. For every five conversations, you get a personal meeting. For every three personal meetings, you set up an interview. For every two interviews, you receive an offer. That means 90 calls can yield an offer. If you make four calls per day, you can earn four offers over the course of 90 days.

This becomes your law of averages. Develop a spreadsheet to track:
- How many calls with no answers/left messages
- How many conversations per day
- How many names received in each conversation
- How many phone conversations created personal meeting
- How many of those meetings set up interviews
- How many interviews resulted in offers
- How many offers resulted before one was accepted

As you develop your averages, you may adjust activity to speed up interviews or slow down interviews.

Important — many candidates fall into the trap of shutting down their networking activities as soon as they begin an interviewing process. They are so certain that their networking efforts are done, they quit doing the things that made them successful. Understand that your first interviews may or may not result in offers. You may accept those offers, or you may turn them down for a number of reasons.

❑ **Redouble your networking efforts while participating in an interviewing process.** Success creates more confidence. Additional confidence creates better results.

❑ Remember your goal is to find positions that you love so much that you are excited to receive compensation for your impacts. You want days to fly by. You want to make positive, measurable impacts and have fun.

❑ Continue to network so you have choices at the end of different interviewing processes.

❑ Intense networking only ends after you start your next position. Then you continue to contribute to your networks but do so outside of Prime Time in consideration for your new employer/business.

❑ Begin a list of references. Decide which references are best to discuss which successful experiences.

Now that you know how, good luck networking!

Prior to discussing the interview process, let's address the importance of internships and co-op programs for college students in their search for their first job.

This is one of those areas in the book where the experienced professionals may move directly to Chapter 6 — "Impressive Interviewing."

CHAPTER 5
BENEFITS OF INTERNSHIPS AND
CO-OPS IN YOUR JOB SEARCH

During the dot-com boom, one of my clients was a very successful Silicon Valley technology firm. One of the founders, an alumnus of Rice University in Houston, Texas, often told me that college recruiting and internships gave his company "access to the brightest and the best minds while we can still afford them." We successfully recruited Rice University graduates for software engineering positions and undergraduates for internships at his firm. We also successfully recruited graduates and undergraduates from Brown University, UCLA, Purdue University and the University of California – Berkeley. One of my responsibilities was to help the client develop its formal internship and co-op programs, and help it to develop a program to house those interns in the extremely expensive Silicon Valley real-estate market.

Today's college students are more astute than the students of the past — and luckier, too. In the past 30 years, internships have evolved into doing real work within the field the student has targeted. Previously, internships may have simply been a filing job in the right area. Because companies are leaner and more filing is done electronically by individuals on the corporate network, companies want interns performing tasks that deliver measurable results. This provides students a wonderful opportunity to apply their knowledge in a work setting.

In the past, colleges and universities required the employer to take time weekly to report in depth on the intern's activities in order to call a job "an internship." That's fine if the supervisor has time; however, most supervisors are already working near their limits. This amount of reporting just discouraged the hiring of interns. Colleges and universities now have adjusted their reporting expectations to encourage the hiring of student interns. Now companies hire interns, teach them how to carry out their tasks and under supervision let them do their job. They expect results. At the end of the internship, there is typically an evaluation.

Students: Understand that you are being evaluated daily as you work. You may not receive the feedback, but the team is constantly observing your work, work ethic and attitude to determine if you are a future fit. They want you to succeed, but if they perceive you as someone with a poor attitude, they will begin to cut their relationship time with you.

What is the value of a summer internship instead of a "summer job"? Sometimes a summer job can pay better than an internship; that is certainly attractive to a student paying her way through college. Generally, those summer positions are construction jobs, restaurant servers or manufacturing line positions.

A summer internship gives the student valuable training and insight in a field of interest. Another important benefit is that a student may decide as a result of that internship that she really is not interested in that field or working at that company. It's better to change fields while in college than wait until you have graduated and are working; you may be able to change your course direction and degree to the new major.

The most important benefit of a successful internship is that the student has decided this is the field for him. He demonstrated his abilities and work ethic to a company that is now interested in hiring him when he graduates. You may call this "Advanced Networking" or "Networking 201."

What is the difference between an internship and a co-op? Generally, a co-op is a more formal program with a specific company. I usually see co-ops used more in the engineering or hard science areas. When you work in a co-op program, beginning in your junior year you will work a semester and attend class a semester. You will be paid for your work, but don't expect full-time compensation. The expectation is that the co-op will give you ever-increasing exposure and responsibilities. It will usually postpone your graduation into the following year. An internship generally occurs during summer breaks, but some are structured to continue as part-time positions or during semester breaks.

At the end of either program, you are either interested in the company and its work or you aren't. If you do a great job (depending on the economy), you will probably receive a job offer. As a candidate, this is the best offer to accept. You know your manager (typically). You know the company and the work. You enjoy working there.

One of my clients was an executive for a financial services company. He began interning at the company the summer of his sophomore year of college. He returned after his junior year and had another successful internship. During his senior year, he was offered a job there following graduation. He grew in the company for 25 years and was a vice president there when we last worked together.

It is not unusual for students to experience that same kind of success using the internship to find a job and later succeeding within the company. Many companies use their internship programs as a recruiting tool. It is a great way to "try out" students to determine if they are a match for the company in all ways:

- Proper skills or the ability to learn them quickly
- Proper cultural fit
- Ability to work as a team member
- Already have experience working with members of team and being accepted as a member of the team (very valuable!)
- Demonstrating the ability to make impacts given the proper corporate training
- "Selling" the student to work for the company by giving them challenging and fun assignments

A recent college graduate who has a successful internship at a com-

pany is more likely to be hired by that company than a student who is applying there without that experience.

This method of recruiting is more valuable than the traditional sourcing and interviewing method. The manager and company truly know the person they are hiring. Additionally, the candidate (student) also knows what to expect. It is a win-win.

Most colleges and universities have a career services or student professional development center on campus. These professionals work very hard to attract well-known and locally attractive companies to recruit on campus. They work with interested students to prepare for their searches for internships and post-graduate jobs. Understand that while software or nursing or sales may be your field of interest, people who work in career services or professional development are passionate about your future success.

Understandably, it is the nature of some students to discount the skills of the career-development professionals. You have been taught to question results and opinions as part of your college education. There is also the adage about the prophet not receiving respect at home. It is not unusual for people to discount the abilities of people they see daily.

Speaking to you as a recruitment professional, I recommend that you heed their advice. They have worked with hundreds or thousands of students and many companies in their years advising students on proper career searches. They have seen the mistakes students have made that negatively affected their job searches. You haven't seen those mistakes, and may be about to make one. Take advantage of their knowledge and experience to accelerate your search.

Career services professionals usually begin to coach freshmen and try to reach them in the first semester of that year. Why so early? Generally, the most attractive internships become available in December and are offered in February. Those companies are trying to identify the "cream of the crop" early so they can lock them into an internship. Internships are more difficult to find between freshman and sophomore years but persistent, convincing freshmen can find them. After sophomore year, companies have more of your college experience to measure your ability to learn (grades) and will question you on your work experience; therefore, sophomores and juniors are more attractive as intern candidates.

Of course you are now saying, "What work experience? How am I expected to get work experience if I need work experience to get it?" Good questions. Did you work in high school or part-time in college? It doesn't need to be in your field of interest. McDonald's, Walmart and Target are proud of the alumni who worked for them while in school. You made an impression on your manager. You know if they are good or bad impressions. Many high school students work very hard in their part-time positions. Others may not be as enthusiastic.

If you worked hard, went above and beyond what was expected and had great attendance, your chances of receiving a positive reference from your current manager goes way up. Keep in mind that some managers are not allowed to provide references or they may be angry that you are considering a move.

When I was consulting on college recruiting with an avionics company, an engineering manager told me, "I will hire a college graduate with a 3.4 GPA who had an appropriate internship before I hire a grad with a 4.0 GPA. Why? If you are only studying, you are expected to earn a 4.0 GPA. I like graduates who work during college because they learn how to perform in the work environment." I cannot improve on that statement.

Now you know "why" to work summer internships while in college. Let's discuss how to find and be hired for an internship.

Obviously, your career services or professional development office is the place to start. Develop a relationship with the professionals in that office early in your college career. Work with them so they know what kinds of internships or co-ops are particularly interesting to you. It would be wise to volunteer with that office during its peak times. They can teach you more about the job-search process, and you never know who you will meet when you are volunteering.

Remember, companies are trying to develop stronger relationships with schools where they had previous success. A representative of the company may be there when you are in the office. You want the career-services staff to recommend you when a company calls and asks for recommendations.

Obviously, listen to the career-services professionals' advice on companies where you should apply for an internship.

- Ask them who has hired interns from your college/university program in the past.

- What kind of experience did those interns have?

- Do your research to determine companies where you would like to intern.

- Ask career services if any of your school's alumni either work at or sponsor internships at those companies.

- Do your parents work in companies that have appropriate internships? Do they know the hiring manager? Can you apply there?

- Find out where recent grads from your program are working and contact them. They often keep their college e-mail addresses for some time after they graduate.

- Establish a professional profile on LinkedIn and search for other alumni at companies that interest you.

- Ask career services if there are older grads from your program who are executives at an appropriate company. They may be willing to create an internship for the right person.

- As you are working this list of suggestions, begin a list of names of people you will network with outside of your college/university.

- Whose parents do you know? Can they help you find an internship in your field?

- If you are active in your religion, go to your religious leader and ask who they know who may be willing to help you find an internship.

If you hit dead ends with these solutions, return to Chapter 4: "Effective Networking to Your Next Position!" and follow those steps. Persistent students prepare and are determined to succeed.

A couple of years ago, I met an industrious college junior who was very interested in an internship with a well-known financial services company. He kept getting noncommittal comments when he asked for his internship status. Finally, one Friday morning he went to the offices. He told security that he was a student who wanted to interview for a summer intern program. As his luck would have it, another student who was offered an internship had just called to decline. This junior was interviewed and received an offer for his internship that day. Timing is everything!

During this process, pretend that you are a consultant offering your services to a firm for the summer. Use all of your different talents to land an interview for your internship. Be creative. Talk with as many people you can.

If you find an internship that does not interest you, either let your career-services office know or go directly to another student that you know may be qualified and interested. Remember, networking is all about helping others in your network.

Now let's discuss your communications skills briefly. I know many college students are trying to replace human contact with texting contact. It can be a timesaver. I am also intimately aware of mobile recruiting applications from the corporate side.

Here is the danger of trying to communicate solely by e-mail and text: neither enables you to efficiently describe the tone of your message. Smiley faces don't cut it in a professional world.

The recruiting/interviewing process is a sales process. The candidates who understand this concept are the ones who are most successful growing their careers. **The sales process is a relationship-building process.** Remember that the hiring process tends to be a cross-generational environment where people of all ages are involved.

The nature of seasoned executives tends to dictate older management. Obviously, there are highly successful young managers — and those managers tend to remain successful throughout their careers. Bill Gates is a wonderful example of a person who was successful at a younger age. Eventually, those successful young managers become successful older managers, and you need to be able to communicate with them at their level in order to be successful with them either as an employee or as a vendor supplying them.

Therefore, take the time to communicate with the managers and human resources professionals directly. If you don't, you run the risk of being eliminated by your competition. Also, no job is truly yours until the day you start. So you need to communicate all the way through the process until your start date. Offers may be rescinded. Do not assume that a hiring manager will accept text messages as a replacement for conversations.

Many times I have observed candidates when I thought one or another was best for the position, and then watched that person lose out when someone else was introduced at the last minute.

Enjoy your internships/co-ops! This is a great way to continue to learn the new workplace and apply the new concepts that you have been taught. Also remember, corporate e-mail systems are not to be used for distributing jokes or pictures. Because they are the property of the company, network administrators may read your e-mail to ensure it is business related. **If these lines saved you from embarrassment or firing, then this book is worth it.**

JOB-SEARCH PROCESS CHECKLIST — Internships/Co-ops

❑ Meet with your career services/professional development services professionals as soon during freshman year as is possible to discuss your current career aspirations.

❑ Work with them to develop a plan to work while in college to develop internships or co-op programs.

❑ Especially during freshman year, offer to volunteer for career services events — for instance, career fairs. You never know who you may meet that may lead to an internship.

❑ Attend the career services meet-and-greet events. Put yourself in a position to be successful.

❑ The best way to find an internship (and later a job) is to network your way to one.

❑ Remember to communicate "the old-fashioned way" with older managers. While it is part of your normal communication skills, not everyone is familiar with or interested in texting. You may be able to "teach" them its advantages, but only after you develop a working relationship with them.

❑ When you interview with managers and human resources, ask for their business cards.

❑ Remember to follow up internship interviews with handwritten thank you notes. Your competition rarely writes thank you notes for interviews. It is a successful best practice for the rest of your career.

❑ Once in your internship, apply yourself enthusiastically and learn everything you can.

Good luck! Enjoy this new experience that will prepare you for your career. Now let's learn how to be an impressive interviewee!

CHAPTER 6
IMPRESSIVE INTERVIEWING

You have now had the opportunity to decide what position you want to target. You have set a goal that stated the job and when you will be working. You have developed your resume so it can be tailored for each position that you are targeting. You have networked and spent a little time responding to Internet postings (no more than 10 percent of your search time), and now you have an interview scheduled!

At the time that the interview is scheduled, ask if the company can send you the application. It is far better to complete the application when you have the information handy — and you are not under the stress of the interview. Tell the truth on your application and in your interview. (Remember the stories in Chapter 3.)

I coach my clients (companies) that recruiting is sales. Now I'm telling you (the candidates) that recruiting is sales! It is important that you understand this concept while searching for a job. What are you selling? You are selling your skills and abilities! If you haven't developed any skills over the years, why would someone want to hire you?

You have worked hard to get to this point. For me, interviewing is fun. I look at it as another networking opportunity where I may be able to help a manager or company benefit from knowing me. I define an interview as a conversation with a purpose — and both sides have the purpose of deciding if this relationship is best for them.

This is a good time to warn you about a typical candidate behavior. **When a candidate schedules an interview, they often stop networking. Never stop networking.** This position may not be the right one. You do not want to have to restart your networking process and lose the momentum you've developed. So set time aside every day to continue your networking efforts. In sales, action begets action; therefore, you may find more opportunities while exploring the first one. Wouldn't it be nice to have several offers to choose from? Remember, you are looking for the job that is so enjoyable that you can't believe they are also paying you!

I have an important little secret for you. As the result of working with several thousand managers since 1981, I can tell you that every single manager has one common feeling regarding interviewing, and it does not matter how skilled they are as an interviewer. **Every single manager is rooting for you to succeed during your interview.** Outside of recruiting teams, most managers dislike the recruiting and interviewing process. They want to spend their time managing their team and making impacts in their fields, not going through dozens of resumes and interviewing strangers. So once they have chosen a slate of candidates to interview, they hope at least one qualifies to work with them. You can understand why they do not want to begin the process again.

Some managers look at this process as an opportunity to improve their team. Those are the great managers who really know how to grow a high-performance team. Their interviews will be strenuous as they try to determine if you have the right skills and attitude.

Therefore, once you have been invited to interview, the odds slightly raise in your favor. Now it is up to you to earn the respect of the manager and/or management team. You earn this respect through preparation for the interview. If you try to skate through an interview, you may just continue skating out the door because you will lose the respect of the manager.

In Chapter 1, I suggested that you develop a skills inventory (those skills that you do well). Prior to an interview, take time to look at the inventory. For every skill with an asterisk, develop a succinct story that relates a time when you successfully used that skill and that may apply to this position and company. Because you spent time researching the company, you have some knowledge of how these skills may be used to make impacts at this new company. Jot a few words down that will help you recall that example. Remember that often managers are taught to ask, "What is your greatest skill/talent?" This list helps you to prepare for those questions.

Why relate a story to demonstrate the skill? There are two major reasons. The first reason is that hiring managers look for proof that you have a skill. Simply responding that you have a skill is not an effective interviewing technique. Generally that response will cause the interviewer to feel that you are trying to avoid the question. The second reason is that **people remember stories.** This is important.

When I was on a recruiting contract with a major telecommunications firm, the managers were interviewing six candidates per day. Many times they later referred to a candidate by "He/she was the candidate that told the story about…"

Research the company as you would if you were going to sell to it. What does its online marketing look like? What do its press releases say? If it is a public company, take a look at its financials. Print a copy of its job description or cut and paste it to your electronic pad. It is important to be an educated candidate. This research helps you develop better questions to ask the hiring manager. For instance, "On your web site, I saw that your company is… How is that going to im-pact your group?" "Is this job description an accurate representation of the job responsibilities?" "What are the three-month, six-month, nine-month and 12-month goals for the position?"

You can learn much about a company before you interview — **knowledge is power.** If you know someone who works there, give her a call to ask if she knows anything about the position or what dem-onstrated skills the manager seeks.

You may decide during your research before the interview that you do not want to interview for them. If that is the case, it is best to make that decision earlier rather than later — and call them to let them know. It's OK. No point to waste people's time. If you decide to make that call, thank them for their time and tell them that you are looking for a position or industry that matches your goals more closely.

This does bring up a point. If you agree to interview, you have made a commitment to that manager, her team and anyone else involved. They have set time aside in their schedules to give you their total focus. **If you decide not to interview with a company for any reason, call and let them know. If you simply don't show, you burn more bridges than you can imagine.**

I introduced a candidate to one of my clients. He was going to interview with the CEO. On the morning of his interview, he did not show. He did not call them nor did he call me. You can imagine my feelings when the CEO called to let me know the candidate didn't show! When I finally reached him, he said that he heard the CEO was a nasty person and he "decided not to interview." I asked why he did not call me or the client. He said that he "didn't feel like it." What bridges do you suppose he burned that day? Obviously, the CEO and any members of the management team who were going to interview him.

About 10 years later, this same candidate approached me to be introduced to my new "sexier" client. After asking him about his experience since I knew him before, I determined that he had not changed nor was his experience directly applicable. Therefore, I did not introduce him to my client. He complained directly to my client that I did not introduce him. When the vice president asked me why I chose not to introduce him, I told her the whole story. She was happy that I did not waste her time with this candidate. Now he had lost credibility with another leader in another company.

It is important to respect people's time whether you respect them or not.

Interview processes differ with each company. When someone calls out of the blue to phone interview you, ask them if you can set up a time for the conversation, even later that day. It will give you time to compose and prepare yourself mentally for the conversation. They understand that you may have something already going on when they call. They may call just to set up a phone screen.

When I am working with clients, particularly if they have a large number of resumes, I suggest that we develop a phone screen to determine who goes to the next level. While you may not interview with the manager in this phone screen, you need to take it seriously. The person conducting this screen is your current gatekeeper — and may be your best advocate. Treat them with respect. The questions they ask can help you get a better sense for the position and the direction of the company. Remember, it is important for you to be an active listener. **Did you realize that when you are paying attention, your brain is actually working harder?** Ask this person about the job description and the accountabilities of the position. Toward the end of the phone screen, ask how you can expect the process to move forward.

Now it is the day of the interview. How do you prepare? Go through all of your notes and the job description. Review the company's press releases to see if there is any late-breaking news that is valuable to you. You may want to add or change one of your short stories.

If you smoke, don't. Nonsmokers can smell smoke on your breath and your clothes. Don't kid yourself. I can smell smoke on clothing, even if you weren't the one smoking. Today, smoking can cost you a job offer. Like it or not, insurance research demonstrates that smokers are sick more often. Companies are allowed to select the candidates who are the best "fit" for their business. You make your own decisions.

If the job is an office or sales job, wear professional clothing: suit, tie, polished shoes. Women should wear conservative jewelry (no dangling earrings) and conservative cosmetics, if you decide to wear either. Beyond earrings, it is best not to show body piercings or tattoos in a professional office for your interview. You have heard this before — you have one opportunity to make a good first impression. It is natural for people to look at your clothing and "accessories" and make judgments regarding your "fit" in an organization. I've heard candidates say, "If they don't like my beard/long hair/tattoos/piercings, that's tough. That's who I am." I accept that line of thinking. Just don't complain if the company feels another person is a better fit for your otherwise perfect job. Remember, the manager also has a right to determine if someone is a fit for their team.

One of my consumer product group clients hired a human-resource generalist. Their corporate culture shuns body piercings and tattoos. They inform candidates during the interviewing process that they are not acceptable. The candidate interviewed without a tongue stud; however, on her first day on the job, she was sporting a tongue stud. The vice president of human resources requested that she remove it. The new employee, who was on a customary 90-day probation, refused to remove it. That was also her last day.

A great book if you have questions about dressing for an interview is John T. Molloy's *New Dress for Success*. I read his earlier book in the 1980s. He actually researched professional dressing and how people reacted to different styles. I have recommended his books to candidates for more than 20 years because they are based on research.

If it is an outside job — construction, for example — wear appropriate, clean business casual clothing to your interview. If the job is one that is with a company that values outdoor experience, wear appropriate clothing for the position.

I worked a career fair once where a candidate told his friends that he was so good and companies were so desperate for candidates, he could even get a job offer if he walked around with a clown costume on. What a schmuck! He even dropped off his resume with companies. No offers for him then — or probably later. His arrogance really stood out. By the way, the companies who received his resume shared his name with other companies.

Dress is important.

Beware of the food that you eat a couple of hours before your interview. Some food can make you gassy.

Once when we were interviewing IT professionals, the IT manager came to my office when her interview with a candidate was over. The manager said, "Don't ever put someone like that in front of me again!" I was startled. The candidate worked for a competitor and on the same types of systems. At that point, we did not know he was failing the technical test. I asked the manager what was wrong with the candidate. It seemed that shortly after he sat down, the poor guy began having gas problems. The manager had to open her windows when he left. Lesson learned.

If you will be even two minutes late, call ahead and tell your connection (HR or the hiring manager). They understand construction, accidents, flat tires, etc. Where did that courtesy go? Everyone has a cell phone now! (Speaking of cell phones, turn it off before you enter the building.) Respect other people and they will respect you.

When you walk into the office for your interview, treat everyone with respect. Period. I generally ask everyone to tell me if the candidate was disrespectful. This is when you should be on your best behavior. Respect the receptionist and act professionally through your interviews. I have had candidates occasionally who felt they were too important to listen to requests the receptionist made. Those actions rarely go unnoticed. The receptionist will let people in the company know if you were not respectful.

Occasionally, you will interview with a company that prefers candidates to complete and sign the application in their office. There have been a number of times when a candidate refused to complete the application when the receptionist presented it. I'm really not sure what one expects to gain from that refusal. It sure isn't going to be a ringing endorsement.

A candidate once did not complete the application prior to the interview as requested. Prior to interviewing him, the HR manager "allowed" him to complete the application at her desk as she waited and worked on e-mail. That was probably a little uncomfortable… I don't believe he received an offer.

No matter your feelings about a company's recruitment processes, you can't do anything about them until you develop credibility inside the company. It is best to follow their processes no matter how backward — or elect to end the process. You do have choices.

Before we go into personal interviews, let's briefly discuss the different formats.

Most candidates are aware of the interview where you sit across the desk from the person interviewing you. It's strictly a "normal" one-on-one interview. The interviewer leads the interview and the candidate follows.

Another potential format is one candidate with a panel of interviewers. This is more stressful for candidates because you may have two or more people asking questions at the same time. How do you handle that format? Apologize to the second manager and focus on responding to one person and question at a time. Once you respond to the first manager's question, turn to the second manager and ask him to please repeat his question. You want to give that question your total focus.

Another potential format is the competitive interview where you have multiple candidates facing multiple interviewers (generally one of whom is a psychologist). While I have never participated in this format, I did suggest it once because I had a bad feeling regarding one of the potential candidates. His ALL CAPS E-MAIL RESPONSE disqualified him; and we didn't have to spend the time interviewing him. The competitive interview attempts to measure both your ability to handle a stressful meeting and at the same time work to create consensus with your responses. The executives look to see if you acknowledge other participants' best responses. They also are trying to get a sense for how you fit into the executive team. It is expensive and time consuming. Some CEOs swear by this format of interview to see how interviewing executives handle the stress of that format and to determine who is the best fit with their team.

For the purpose of keeping things simple, let's focus on the more common one-on-one interview, possibly with several managers scheduled to meet with you. While you are in the lobby, check your cell phone one more time to ensure it is off.

There are different methods to interview candidates within different formats. To prepare you for these interviewing techniques, let's explore the different types of methods that you may experience.

- Much has been written about behavioral interviewing. Some companies attempt to design the entire interview as a behavioral interview. People are wonderfully consistent. When backed into a corner, we attempt to solve a problem in the same manner with which we found success in the past. The interviewer anticipates challenges the new employee will face in this position and structures a question that can give insight about how the candidate will handle the situation.

- For instance, let's assume that this is a call-center manager position with angry clients who ask to escalate unsatisfactory answers. This is a potential line of behavioral questions for a candidate with call-center experience: "When you were a manager at XYZ Services Co., how did you handle angry clients who wanted to escalate a problem up the chain of responsibility? Can you give me a couple of examples when you were able to satisfy the client?" After you respond they may ask, "Obviously, it is difficult to satisfy everyone. Please give me an example of a situation when you weren't able to satisfy the client. Describe the situation, the actions that you took and the results. What did you learn from that situation?" You can tell that they are trying to determine how you will respond to those clients once you start working there.

- A follow-up question generally is the most effective way to probe a candidate's response to a behavioral question. There are several methods to probe the response. One way is to compliment them. "Congratulations on handling that very difficult situation! What experience from your past did you draw from to decide to take that path?"

- Occasionally, it is good for the manager to change the line of questioning by asking a probing type of question where the interviewer is looking for a what, when, where or who response. For instance, "Where were you working when you were trained to handle conflict?"

- Generally, it is best if the manager pays attention to your response to any question; however, asking a follow-up question to your answer of the probing question can provide more information that leads to understanding your motivations. An example follow-up question could be, "If you were receiving such valuable training at that company, why did you choose to leave?"

- I train hiring managers to ask open-ended questions. Sometimes a yes or no response is fine. Usually they are looking for more information, so they structure a question that requires you to give more information. They may want to see how much information you have absorbed in your research and interview, so they ask, "What positive, measurable impacts do you feel you could make in this position?"

- One of my favorite techniques to use with sales professionals is to be silent after they respond, then nod my head or move my hand as if to say, "Please continue..." Then I see how much more information they will give me. *On several occasions, the sales candidate continued to talk for 20 minutes without asking me for a clarification. One candidate reached the 20-minute point and stopped dead in his tracks. He looked at me and said, "I just blew this interview, didn't I?"* When you find yourself in this situation, simply ask the interviewer what additional information they are looking for, so your response may be focused to their need for information. An interview is not the time to enter the confessional, especially unknowingly.

- There are times that the interviewer may repeat some of the words from your response in order to elicit a response. Your response to why you left a position could be, "I just didn't feel that my professional impacts were appreciated." The interviewer may respond, "Professional impacts?" They are actually giving you an opportunity to talk about your impacts and at the same time are developing a better understanding of your motivations.

- When a manager wants to understand more about specific positions or situations that you have worked, she may ask you to compare one position or project to another. "You said that the sale to XYZ Company was one of the most complicated sales you have closed. How did that compare to the one with ABC Company? How were they different? What did you learn from each sale?"

- When your resume contains broad statements regarding skills, you should expect a hiring manager to ask for examples to prove that you have those skills. Remember when you were building stories to demonstrate those skills in our first chapters? Now you apply that lesson and give the best example from your repertoire of responses that suits their needs. For instance, perhaps in your resume you mentioned that you had "excellent management skills." What does that mean? In comparison to whom? Tell your story that discusses the successes of the people that you have managed.

It is important to be able to discuss your identified strengths and tell stories that demonstrate success with those skills. Try to pick skills that would make positive impacts in that position. It is also important to discuss areas that you need to improve and what you are doing to improve those skills. For instance, you may be terrified speaking to a group. You have identified that as an area for improvement, so you join a local Toastmasters group to practice and improve that skill. Managers appreciate the fact you know where you need improvement and have taken the initiative to improve.

One client asked me to train a talented new human-resource representative how to interview. We chose an executive administrative assistant position that reported to a fairly tough sales vice president. The rep combed through the resumes that we had sourced and picked the three she thought were best. When I looked at the stack, I concurred. She set up the appointments for the three candidates.

When each of them arrived, she introduced me to them. I mentioned that I was coaching the rep to improve her interviewing skills. I was going to be on the other side of the conference room table from them. If we went through the entire interview without my asking a question, that was great. If I did ask a question, it was because I needed additional clarification.

The first two candidates and the rep did just fine. I did not feel the need to speak up. The third candidate was doing well until she was asked what her weakness was. The candidate said, "My weakness is that I like people too much." Well, that was the first time that I ever heard that as a weakness, so she received my full attention. She then went on to make her weakness a strength.

The rep was going to let her move forward. I decided to probe a little deeper. I excused myself and said, "Well, we were looking more for a skill you needed to improve. What you did was turn your weakness into a strength. I recognize that approach in interview coaching. Can you tell me what area you need to improve?" She responded that, "Another weakness is that I..." and proceeded to turn it into a strength. I responded that I understood how she was taking some attribute, discussing it as a weakness and then demonstrating positive results from that action or attitude.

Trying one more time, I asked, "This is an important support position to a vice president of sales. Are there any software classes where you would like to improve skills or any other area we could help you improve skills?" Her response? "I am NOT a weak person!" She was right! However, she did not listen, either. I apologized profusely and turned the conversation back over to the rep. The rep recognized that the interview was essentially over at that point since we found her fatal flaw.

Remember that people remember stories. When you stop reading this book, will you remember all of the principles that we discussed? Probably not. Will you remember the stories? The ones that resonated with you will probably remain in your memory for a while; therefore, prepare to tell the stories that best represent your skills and abilities to get the job done.

Take the time to practice answering these different types of questions. Have someone ask you different questions from all of the different interviewing techniques. Just as a shortstop in baseball practices fielding each type of grounder, line drive and pop-up time and again so they are confident in a game, practice interviewing so you can recognize what the interviewer is looking for in your response. A key way to build a relationship with a hiring manager and team is to demonstrate confidence during your interview.

Here comes your first interviewer. Approach with confidence, appropriate eye contact and a friendly smile. Give them a firm handshake — don't break their fingers, just firm. Never give anyone a wet fish handshake! Yuck! It just says so many bad things about you — lack of confidence is among them. It used to surprise me when a woman gave me a firm handshake. Now women seem to be taught the importance of a firm handshake and do so more consistently than some men.

Appropriate eye contact means to look directly at the interviewer, but this is not a staring contest. A nice friendly smile is appropriate. It is fine to accept an offer of water. Water is nice because it can help settle your throat should it tighten. Remember that coffee may leave your mouth dry and with that nasty used coffee smell.

When you go into the office or conference room, wait until your interviewer indicates where you should take a seat before sitting. Once I had a manager candidate that I was interviewing go behind the desk when we entered the office. I smiled and said, "I can see what side of the desk you are used to sitting." He laughed and said, "Oops!" He was fine. I let him remain in that seat for our interview. We offered the job and he accepted. Generally, it is better that the interviewer gestures toward the appropriate seat.

When you have a cup or container of water, ask for a coaster before placing it on a desk. It's not good form to stain a nice desk, but you would be remembered…

In preparation for your interviews, visualize the potential structure of your interview. There generally is a warm-up period. It is followed by the meat of the interview, and then the point where the manager has made a decision and asks if you have any further questions. If you are paying attention during your interview, you may sense when you are moving into the different phases. Many times you may know if the manager is definitely interested in you. The manager may just tell you so and ask when you can start. They may be more subtle, but still let you know there is interest in your candidacy.

When I present "The Secrets of a Successful Job Search," I tell the audience that a good interview is like a racquetball game. Prior to playing a racquetball game, you have a short warm-up session. It gives an experienced player an opportunity to test the opposing player. Just as in the racquetball warm-up, the first questions in the interview are very easy — "Tell me a little about your experience." Generally the interviewer asks this question while they are reading your resume (sometimes for the first time). This is an appropriate time to use your "Here I Am!" speech. Then they may ask a little about your most-recent job. Now that you are warmed up, a skillful interviewer will begin the behavioral questions mixed in with the specific skill questions.

One or more of the questions may be directed toward your relationship with your previous managers. If you are so inclined, this would be a great opportunity to absolutely nail them. Don't do it! Just be happy to characterize your relationship as "professional." If you say negative things about a previous manager, what happens?

The hiring manager wonders if the problem was the manager or you. Then they wonder what you will say about them in a couple of years; this is not the path you want them on. Don't lie and say you had a wonderful relationship if it wasn't. Remember, the previous manager may be called as a reference. When the previous manager asks the hiring manager how you characterized the relationship and the reply is "professional," they will probably return the favor.

Remember to ask good, informed questions based on your notes and based on what the manager has told you.

I once worked with a senior manager who laid out a situation in her interview. If the candidate did not ask a specific question, she would not extend an offer to them. You need to be an active listener. (She never shared with me the specific question). If you can focus on the hiring manager and their questions, it is a good idea to jot down some notes. These may help you develop questions. Remember, if you do not understand how an organization is set up or why a company has a specific process or why something that you heard sounded wrong, ask the interviewers a question to clarify your thinking. That is more than OK; it is expected.

Part of your job during the interview is to attempt to build a professional relationship with the people who conduct the interview. Remember, if someone is interviewing you, they generally have input on whether or not you will be hired. Most hiring managers want to feel that you will jump into their canoe and paddle upstream with them if they need that support. You build that relationship through active listening and asking good questions — and through the stories you relate that demonstrate you have done this in the past.

Look at pictures and certificates or degrees on their office wall. Imagine your good fortune if you happen to note they graduated from the same college as you. This gives you an immediate relationship with them.

During the interview, it is a good idea to take notes. Focus on the challenges and where you may be able to make impacts. It is good to discuss an area where it is critical for you to make an impact. Once you feel the manager is comfortable that you will make that impact, ask him if he agrees that you will be able to make progress there. This reinforces in his mind that he has found someone who can help solve his problems. Isn't that what people are paid for — solving problems? If he agrees, then write it down. If not, you now know that you must overcome that objection before you receive an offer. Ask if you can return to that question or situation and discuss it further. At this point you are consulting with him. Ask for more information and then use an experience from your past that demonstrates you can make that impact or know how to solve the problem.

Your posture during an interview is very important. If you lean back in your chair, it appears you lack interest in the conversation. Sit toward the edge of your chair and sit straight up. **When you make a point, lean forward to demonstrate the importance of that point.** This action also demonstrates your confidence in making it. Over the years, many candidates have lost opportunities because managers felt they were either lazy or not interested. Their posture gave the bad impression.

I alluded to asking the hiring manager what the three-month, six-month, nine-month, and 12-month goals were for the position. Why do you want this information?

1. The skills necessary to be successful in that position in the first year become crystal clear.

2. The title of the position and the job description do not give you the level of information you need in order to decide if the position truly interests you.

3. The goals give you and the manager an opportunity during the interview to discuss the challenges he expects you to overcome. They also give you the opportunity to demonstrate you have the ability to do the job successfully. If you feel they have questions regarding your ability to do this job, and you feel one of your references can answer those questions for both of you,

feel free at this point to offer their name and phone number to discuss your experience at a previous company. Let your reference know to expect the call and why someone is calling.

4. During your meetings after you are hired, you may use these goals to discuss progress and challenges and to ask for advice. At your annual review, there should be no surprises for either of you.

Once I was doing some career counseling with a CFO. As we were discussing the interview and salary-negotiating process, I suggested that he mention that until he knew what the accountabilities were for the CFO position, he could not put a value on the position. He replied that if he interviewed a CFO and she didn't know what the accountabilities were for that position, he would show her the door. My reply? "So, what you are saying is the responsibilities for the CFO position for General Electric are the exact same as the CFO position at a telecom startup — and both positions have the exact same accountabilities as those in a financially troubled firm?" Of course they are not. Every company has expectations for a position that may differ slightly from another company or industry — and the position title is the same. **This is why it is important for you to really understand the goals and accountabilities for each position when you interview.**

As you interview, you are measuring the company, the hiring manager and the position in real time. Once both of you have completed your interview, you probably know your level of interest. This is a great time to tell the hiring manager that you are interested in the position because "I feel… (Give them some solid reasons regarding the job duties, the manager's management style and/or the company's culture)." As you leave (if you are interested in the position), it is a good time to ask, "Is there anything that would prevent you from offering this position to me?" Why do you ask that question? If you are interested in the job, that question will tell you if there is information that you need to explain, either in a different way or in a bit more detail, and satisfy the hiring manager's objection.

You know you just had a great interview when you emerge from the interview sweating and smiling!

Once you get 15 to 20 minutes away from the interview, you will be-gin to remember aspects of the conversation that I refer to as the "Wish I Would Have Saids." Find a quiet place — whether it is a fast food res-taurant, a nice restaurant where you can order a soda or coffee, or even a library — to sit down and make some notes about your conversation/conversations. This is an important exercise for a couple of reasons.

1. Most people cannot prepare so completely for an interview as to be prepared to give the best examples for each skill within the context of a new company.

2. If you do not write them down, I guarantee that you will re-member that you had "Wish I Would Have Saids," but to save your life, you can't remember a single one. If you get a second interview with the company, this new information should be mentioned. It can mean the difference between an offer or not. If there is no second interview, this information may be used for negotiation if a lower-than-expected offer is extended. We will cover that in the salary negotiation chapter coming up.

3. Finally, do you really want to separate yourself from the other candidates? **Sit down and handwrite a personal thank you note to each person who participated in the interview.** Unfortunate-ly, today most candidates forget that common courtesy. People remember when you take this extra step.

Now let's discuss how to impress with your references.

A very strong reference can make the difference between receiving an offer that you will absolutely accept and not receiving an offer. Enlightened companies and hiring managers understand the impor-tance of an effective reference check.

Don't let people tell you that reference checking is dead. Too many times I've heard managers say the reference check is a waste of time. Legally, it may be regaining importance as the final due diligence be-fore hiring a candidate; therefore, it is important to be able to contact a number of people who can discuss you as an employee or differ- ent skills you have demonstrated. Companies usually require three professional references who can intelligently discuss your professional abilities. If you are a college recruit and have not worked part-time during college, they may take references from professors or a person- al reference from someone who has known you for a long time.

I once interviewed a female programmer/analyst. Her responses demonstrated that she knew what she was doing professionally. She offered me several refer- ences. So I called her most recent reference, a female manager, and mentioned that the candidate had given me her name as a reference. When the manager burst out laughing, I thought, "That's not a good sign!"

The manager asked me if I had met the candidate in person. I replied that I had. She said, "You probably noticed that she was gorgeous." I replied that I did. The manager said she had hired the candidate. She was very talented; however, after working there for a short period of time, she began to date one of her co- workers. After an intimate relationship that lasted several months, she broke off the relationship — and began dating another co-worker. Evidently, she whis- pered some of her previous relation's interesting preferences to her new friend.

Shortly after, the manager found the two males fist fighting in the hall over this woman. All three were looking for new jobs after the fight.

Obviously this was not a person I would introduce to a client. Be sure to check with your references prior to giving their names to a potential employer. If they are excited to be a reference, that's a great sign. If they are reticent, it's best to move on.

It is a good idea to coach a reference just prior to the call from either a manager or human resources representative. How do you coach a reference? As an active listener during your interview, you generally can tell if the manager is concerned about your ability to perform one or more of the required duties of a position. Suggest to the reference that they bring up a specific success that you had while working with them to demonstrate that skill. References appreciate this type of guidance. Otherwise, they are trying to remember examples that may be several years or more in the past.

The references that you choose to discuss your abilities should be people who have seen you successfully perform related, required duties while working with them; therefore, one reference may be able to discuss your management capabilities. Another reference may be able to focus on your technical abilities. (In this case, "technical" means your day-to-day functions, whether you are a nurse, recruiter, CFO, writer, mechanic or software engineer.) The final reference may focus on your strategic abilities (project planning, long-term planning, budgeting, etc.). Management references are best. Sales or sales-support professionals may want to use one or more clients as references. Just be careful if this is a confidential search.

When you forward your references for a position, note where the person may be able to give the best feedback on your abilities. This information will help coach the person conducting the reference check. Obviously, all references need to be able to discuss your fit within their organizations and whether they would hire you again.

Once you reach this point in the series of processes, you are nearing a successful conclusion to your search.

For a list of potential interview questions, see Appendix B beginning on page 127.

JOB-SEARCH PROCESS CHECKLIST — Impressive Interviewing

❑ Your skills assessment is done; however, it is a dynamic document that may change according to your memory and the jobs you locate.

❑ Your base resume is completed. You change your resume to reflect the needs of each company that you either apply to or interview with.

❑ **You continue to network and grow your networking contacts — especially after you have set up interviews.** Keep your networking momentum going!

❏ In preparation for each interview (even second interviews with the same company), research the company and review your notes. What challenges can you help it overcome?

❏ You have reviewed the different interviewing formats.

❏ You have practiced the different interviewing methods in order to be confident in your responses to different styles of questions.

❏ You checked to ensure your cell phone is off. It is embarrassing when it rings during an interview. If you answer it, you probably will not receive an offer.

❏ **Remember to ask the manager about the three-month, six-month, nine-month and 12-month goals early in the conversation.**

❏ You have developed responses to both your strengths and weaknesses questions.

❏ As the interview is coming to completion, you tell the manager that you are interested in the position — and why.

❏ Prepare a list of potential references prior to your interview. Some may be former managers. Others may be able to discuss certain technical skills (nursing procedures, sales skills, programming skills, etc.)

❏ Prepare for the interview by reviewing the list of potential interview questions in Appendix B.

❏ After your conversation, go somewhere quiet and list your "Wish I Would Have Saids." These are better examples than the ones you used during the interview. You may use these examples in second interviews and salary negotiations.

This is a natural segue into the next chapter — Chapter 7: "The Art of Salary Negotiation."

CHAPTER 7
THE ART OF SALARY NEGOTIATION

Congratulations! You have overcome the other painful aspects of your search to reach the point of discussing compensation. While some people actually enjoy negotiating compensation with a potential new employer, this is generally an uncomfortable area for most people, especially if their jobs did not require negotiating skills. What is your service worth to a new company?

Every company is different, even in the same industry. Many value positions differently. Salary negotiation is also an area where executives have more leverage than most mid-level or entry-level candidates. I include a negotiating script later in this chapter that may benefit an executive more than a mid-level manager, but you may certainly try it at all levels. College recruits usually have little opportunity to negotiate beyond some money for relocation expenses.

By the way, keep networking throughout your salary-negotiation process. Until both sides are happy with your offer, it is not done. One or the other side may step away from the negotiations; therefore, keep networking until you start your first day. At this point you are saying, "I should keep networking after we negotiated an offer that I accepted?" Yes. You cannot control the economy or terrorist attacks or other potential impacts on a company. I have had candidates call me the day they were supposed to start with a new company, only to discover the company had a downturn and could not hire them on their start date. Generally, that does not happen at the executive level because of potential lawsuits, but I have seen it happen several times at mid-level and technical positions.

In the first chapter, I covered taking stock of your skills. Later, we discussed the importance of including your impacts in your resume and interview. Some people told me that "I just did my job. I don't have any impacts."

If you "just did your job," of course you made impacts! Companies do not hire people to take up space and salaries. One hopes you did the best job you could. For instance, let's say you were a cashier. When you are finished with your shift, does your cash drawer balance every time? Isn't that a positive, measurable impact? You can talk about being detail-oriented and dependable, qualities that every hiring manager seeks. Wouldn't it be cool to be able to say that "my cash drawer balanced every day for the past four years?"

Even some overly modest C-level executive candidates have made that comment to me about "just doing my job" during the distress immediately following a reduction in force. They should discuss their successful strategic decisions, how their cost-cutting suggestions added profits to the bottom line, how their inspired leadership led to an engaged workforce. One place to look for your impacts is your old annual or board reviews.

Therefore, it doesn't matter whether you are an executive or a cashier. The complexity of the work is the difference between the jobs. Both levels of work are important to the successful company.

"When do you feel that salary negotiation begins?" is a question that I ask during my salary-negotiation presentation to candidates. My feeling is that salary negotiation begins when the company decides to open a position and gives compensation for that position a budget number. The company now has a level of compensation that demonstrates how it values the position. It is the range they are willing to pay for that work.

This is a good time to remind you that a company places a certain value on a position. You may feel you may be worth more or need more but to that company the position is worth only what they budgeted. Many times a person has shared with me that their spouse wanted to be a stay-at-home parent, and therefore they "needed" more money. Actually, your financial situation is not the company's issue. It is yours.

Don't begin that conversation with a representative of the company or your recruiter. That discussion raises questions on your judgment.

Some companies will require a candidate to put compensation requirements in a cover letter when a resume is submitted. This is one of their screens. I ask every candidate about salary requirements to see whether I feel they are "reasonable." After so many years in the recruitment industry, I generally have a pretty good feel for current salary ranges for most positions. In this chapter, you will learn how to handle those compensation/salary requests.

Let's get back to discussing compensation conversations. As a candidate, it is important to understand the value that a company puts on a job. If you were contributing at a high level within a large company, you may be surprised how the value may change in a smaller company. In some smaller companies, your value may be substantially higher. Whereas in another company, they may feel that you were over-compensated. You may think it's a minefield out there; however, there are ways to navigate/manage through it.

Many companies do not understand that "recruiting is sales." You can use that to your advantage. Most recruiters do not want to waste their time. **If they ask you what you were making at a previous job, respond by asking "What is the compensation/salary/hourly range for this position?"** Many times their response will save everyone time. Simply put, if the company does not value the work produced by this position, you either have a wonderful opportunity to prove them wrong or you may have a situation that will provide you with many frustrating days if your work is not valued.

For instance, I once received a call from a recruiting firm asking if I would be interested in a contract-recruiting consulting assignment in Des Moines. I said, "Sure." Then I asked the hourly rate the client was willing to pay. She replied, "$17.50 per hour." I chuckled and told her I hadn't worked for so little since the 1970s. Obviously, they did not value recruiting very highly. If you pay for a clerk, that's probably what you'll get.

Hourly workers have less room for negotiation than higher-compensated salaried workers.

A way for anyone to begin a salary negotiation is to ask, "Is there any flexibility in the offer?" They may say, "Why do you ask?" If they do, they have cracked open the door for a discussion to increase the offer. Then you may mention some of your "Wish I Would Have Said" comments from your review of the interview. Then ask if they might be willing to increase the offer base or give a signing bonus. Sometimes companies are willing to give an extra week of vacation or increase the relocation package if that is required. Don't expect a large increase in your base compensation. They usually have extended an offer that is within a range in their budget or comparable to others in similar positions in their company.

If the person who is extending the offer says it is their final offer, you have a decision to make. As a result of your interviews with them, do you feel they are going to promote you if you do a great job and make positive measurable impacts? If the answer is yes and the offer is close to your requirements, then you may decide to accept.

If the answer to that question is no, then you should think hard about declining, but do so in a positive manner and ask that they get back to you if another position opens where you may be able to make impacts. As the RecruiterGuy, I have had several experiences where the company realized that a candidate turned out to be the right one, realized the offer was too low and came back with a higher compensation package. That doesn't happen often, but it does happen.

Negotiation is an art, not a science. Most important, remember not to take the negotiations personally. While I realize that it is personal to you and your family, remember that essentially you are "selling" your services to the new company; therefore, this is a sales situation and objectivity is important. Don't be afraid to walk away from an offer that is too low. It obviously is the wrong position for you. We don't work all of these hours just to be frustrated in our job. Again, if they do not value the position highly enough to pay your worth, you will be frustrated almost daily.

Please do not fall into the trap of asking "for a week to think about an offer" that you know you are going to accept. What do you gain by doing that? What do you lose? They may feel you will accept but keep looking. That's not a positive way to begin a working relationship. On the other hand, what happens when you accept that same offer immediately? You send a message to your future manager and company that you are excited about working with them. Isn't that the way to begin your professional relationship?

Now I am going to touch on a sensitive subject. Even if you are religiously devout, it is best if you do not say that you are going to "pray on this offer." If that is the case, hopefully you have been praying through the whole process. God probably has already indicated whether it is right for you. You just need to listen. The reason I mention this topic is that I have received that response more than you would believe over the years. If you insist on responding in that fashion, the result may be that the company will find a way to rescind the offer because you concerned them that you may spend time proselytizing during work hours, not working; or worse yet, simply cannot make a decision. Just say, "I'm excited about your offer. May I get back to you tomorrow?" Keep it simple.

Once you accept the offer, honor your commitment. When an offer is accepted, a company stops all recruiting on that position. The manager is excited that you accepted and has probably already penciled you into some projects or scheduled you to work. If you change your mind, they must begin recruiting from the beginning, and that may put the manager months behind. Obviously, you should never expect to work with them in the future because your integrity is now called into question.

If you are employed, it is best to give two weeks' notice. It is the expectation of your current employer. You never want to burn bridges.

The Salary-Negotiation Script

Before I go through the salary-negotiation script with you, understand that while it has been proven effective, when dealing with people and their emotions, nothing works 100 percent of the time. Pay attention not only to what the other person says but how they say it. If you sense they are not receiving it well, you may need to change your direction, or decide that you may not want to work with them. Too often, the human resources representative is young and inexperienced and may be defensive. The seasoned HR executive generally will be fine.

If you are an executive, you may be interviewing with either the board of directors or the executive management team. They understand how to negotiate and probably will be a little disappointed if you don't try to negotiate a better package.

Review the example of the executive in the book's introduction who used this script to secure a much larger offer than he expected.

Now we can discuss the script.

After the company budgets for the position, what is the next step in the salary-negotiation process? Generally, someone representing the company will call you for an initial phone screen and level-of-interest measurement. They usually will ask your current compensation or your desired level of compensation. It is best to sidestep this question by asking, "What is the range on this position?" If it is too low, you may just thank them for their interest and mention that if another position opens at a higher level, "Please contact me."

If they pressure you for a number, just respond that every company is different and every job has different responsibilities, therefore, "Let's not get the cart ahead of the horse. Let's determine if I have the required skills to make positive impacts and if I fit your culture. Once we have those issues settled, I am certain we can reach an agreement on a fair level of compensation." Remember, you may be measured during this time on your ability to negotiate for the company.

Companies operate in different ways during the process. Some may require executive-level candidates to complete an application. Others may not. If they require you to complete an application, you are facing the next opportunity for the company to find your compensation requirements. Most applications have a space titled "Salary Requirement."

How do you handle the "Salary Requirement" space on an application? Easy. Simply write or type "Open." It is easy to remember, hard to misspell and does not lock you into a number. Do not write "Negotiable" for a couple of reasons.

I have seen "negotiable" misspelled every conceivable way over the years.

"Negotiable" usually does not fit the space well, which forces you to shorten it to "Neg" or "Negot." (The company doesn't want you writing really big numbers in that space!)

If you decide to write a number in the space, only one good thing can happen and two bad things can happen — not good odds. The only possible good thing that can happen is for the manager to complete the interview and say to you, "Margaret (or Mason), wow this must be a meeting of the minds; $101,256 is *exactly* what we were going to offer you!" If people can't successfully guess the right number between 1 and 10, how do you expect them or you to guess exactly the right number, especially when we're talking five-, six- or seven-figure incomes?

What are the two bad things that can happen? One is that you may overshoot what they are willing or able to pay for a base, therefore eliminating yourself from the competition. They may have been willing to give you a competitive base and a piece of the company if you were the right level and able to create the right results. If your research showed they had a tremendous potential like Google in their early years, you may have been willing to accept that challenge.

The other bad thing that could happen is that they may have been willing to give you a larger package than you wrote in "Salary Requirement." Because you wrote a lower number, they want to make you happy and that could be your offer. That gives you a weak negotiating stance because it's the number you gave them.

Back in the 1980s, I was working with a technology professional coming out of the military. He was a sharp guy. Because he was in the military, his salary was a little lower than normal — in the low $30,000s. During our conversations, we agreed that he would allow me to conduct his salary negotiations. I then proceeded to discuss this salary-negotiation education with him. Prior to his interview, I negotiated a salary of $42,000 with the manager should he pass his in-terview and technical skills. During his interview, he completed the application. In "Salary Requirement" he wrote "$35,000" as his expectation. Guess what? The manager wanted to make him happy and she saved her budget $7,000 in the first year alone. It took him four years to get to the level I negotiated for him prior to his interview.

The application also has another area where the company may qualify your compensation — your job history. In most applications, they ask for your starting and ending compensation or salary. When completing this area, place an * in those spaces. **At the bottom of the page, write "* Will be willing to discuss at the appropriate time during the interview." Actually, you never really want to discuss these numbers because it is your private financial information.**

The one field where you may be required to give this information is sales. Unfortunately, some sales professionals have a history of inflating their numbers, especially commissions. Be prepared to show management your W-2 from the previous year.

Once you have completed your application and handed it in, the human resource professional will generally glance through it to ensure you have filled all open spaces. When they see that you wrote "open" in the "Salary Requirement" space, they usually ask you what "open" means. Here is your response (understand that I know you will change this script to better fit your personality or the position, but keep all of the elements):

"Until I meet with the manager or board and truly know:

- what the job entails;

- what you expect from me;

- what positive, measurable impacts I can make;

- and where I can grow within the company over the next five years, then I cannot make an intelligent assessment on a fair level of compensation. Let's move on with the interview so we can get those questions answered."

Isn't that statement correct? Without that information and understanding of the challenges and potential impacts, how do you assign a compensation number to a position? Additionally, it is important for you to get a sense for how the company values this position.

This script also gives both you and the manager a platform for your interview if the manager asks you what "open" means. Even if they don't hear your script, you can use it as a base of the conversation.

During your interview, it is important to get agreement on where they feel you may be able to make measurable impacts. Make note of these on a separate page in your notepad.

Once your interview is over, the manager or board member may say, "Now you know what the job entails, what we expect from you, where you may be able to make impacts and where you may be able to grow within the next five years. What is your assessment of a fair level of compensation?"

If you are truly interested in the position, your response should follow these lines: "I am really interested in your position because of what the job entails (mention some things about what the job entails that are attractive to you) and what you expect from me (mention those areas that excite you). Can we chat briefly about the potential impacts I can make?" Here, go over your list of agreed impacts, reinforcing that you are an impact performer. Finally, discuss the positive side of the potential future growth.

Then say, "As a result of my interview(s) you have a much better feel where I fit into your corporate compensation structure than I will ever have. I am very interested in this position. Please make me the best offer that you can and I will sincerely consider it."

This gives you a salary-negotiation strategy. The first party that puts a number on the table loses negotiation leverage. **This script enables you to push salary negotiation where it belongs — when both parties indicate an interest in each other.**

As I mentioned in Chapter 6 on "Impressive Interviewing," once you get 15 to 20 minutes from your interview, sit down in a quiet place and jot down your "Wish I Would Have Saids." These are the better examples of your experience and past impacts that you should have used during the interview. They may be introduced in your salary negotiation if an offer is extended.

After a successful interview where both sides indicate interest in each other, you may receive a call to return so they can extend you an offer in person. Or, they may choose to call you to extend an offer over the phone. Different companies handle offers in different ways. If a third-party recruiter is involved, the recruiter strongly prefers to extend the offer. Sometimes, a human resource professional will extend the offer. In other companies, the hiring manager makes the call to extend an offer.

Many times, companies will extend a contingent offer prior to completing their due diligence of reference checking and drug test results. The offer is contingent upon the successful completion of those items. Executives may need to go through a credit check, particularly if they handle or have access to corporate money.

Up until now, have we negotiated a salary? No. We've just negotiated whether you would tell them your salary requirements and created a foundation for your interview.

When you receive your offer, if you are going to try to negotiate a higher base, bonus, options, higher relocation benefits, etc., now is the time to ask, "Do you have any flexibility in your offer?" There will probably be one of two answers.

They may say something along the lines of, "You asked us to give you our best offer. This is it." Now you have a decision to make. Is this the right position and right company for me?

As we covered earlier, however, they may say, "Why do you ask?" If they ask that question, the door is cracked open for you to reply, "I am very interested in this position and working with you (or the manager or board). I was hoping for a larger package. Additionally, while I was reviewing our conversation, there were a few examples that better demonstrate the impacts I could make here. Could we spend a few minutes chatting about them?"

If you are asking for additional compensation, remember it is a good idea to give the company additional information on which to base their decision. Otherwise, it is very easy for them to say that their compensation decision was based on the information you gave them.

Companies typically will not increase the base compensation offer by a large percentage because they do not want to negatively impact their compensation ranges. They do have other ways to increase your compensation for this year, particularly if you must accept a cut in your base.

The first way a company may supplement your base income is to offer a signing bonus. This allows you to earn the same or more than you did at your last job without impacting their base compensation. Next budget year, they can decide to raise the compensation bands or give you a promotion (if deserved). Generally, the signing bonus is given on your first day. Some companies will hold all or a portion of your bonus until you work past the probationary period.

Another way that companies can add income is by adding a week or so of paid vacation to your package. This is a particularly attractive alternative for people who like to travel or treasure their days off. The key is to actually take the time off.

Some companies will offer quarterly and annual bonuses. When I worked for a startup as a manager, I was constantly amazed when I was paid a bonus and the company was not showing a profit; however, I did accept the check. These bonuses generally are based on the individual and the company hitting certain measurable targets.

After all of the Alternative Minimum Tax (AMT) issues where people lost their homes, stock options lost much of their popularity. Now, because Congress never bothered to index AMT to inflation in the 1980s or since, it is beginning to impact middle income families. Congress will neither repeal nor change the law. So if a company offers you stock options and it appears that the company is ready to grow quickly, talk to your tax accountant about protecting yourself and then decide whether or not to accept them.

Depending on your position, some companies will offer a car. Again, just understand the potential tax impact.

Finally, if you have to move, the relocation package may be an area that can have a positive impact on your decision. Few companies are willing to buy houses these days, at least at a price that people are willing to accept. Many people are not able to sell at the house's current ap-praised value. There are other areas where you may be able to increase your relocation package. Possibly have the company pack and move you instead of just moving you.

Once we were packed by a moving company. I made the bad mistake of leaving my suitcase with my clothes for the trip and my next day at the office in my bedroom. I told three people not to pack it. When someone called me out to our garage to ask if we were taking or leaving something, my suitcase must have fit perfectly in a box. When I returned, the suitcase was packed — and probably already on the truck. Next time, anything that I don't want packed will be in my rental car before they arrive. I had to buy clothes, toiletries and an inexpensive duffle to get through the next two days.

Regarding your relocation package, ask if they can bump it up for tax purposes. Otherwise much of the money you were counting on for your move will go to taxes.

If you are moving middle school- or high school-age children, ask the new company if the kids can accompany you on your first house-hunting trip. The children may yell and scream, but they are more flexible than you give them credit. They just want some say in their move; therefore, set up meetings with principals or curriculum specialists and coaches, drama teachers, music teachers, (any other special-interest professionals), etc., prior to your house-hunting trip. In your request for the meeting, coach the individual to address the children, not you. Set these meetings to give them a choice of school districts if you can. Then look for housing in the school district the children select. **Your move will be easier if your children are also "recruited" to the new area.**

If your spouse works and will need to find a job in the new area, ask for job-search help for your spouse. It can be formal or informal help. Depending on your spouse, networking may be difficult in a new area. Any introductions your company can make will certainly help with acceptance of the move.

During the same move that I described above, my wife interviewed at two hospitals in the new city during our house-hunting trip. It gave her a sense for the area and her potential employment opportunities. After returning to Maryland, she received an offer from one of those hospitals. Her acceptance of that offer made her feel better about our move.

Therefore, your salary negotiations may include the request for benefits that you have not considered.

Caution: if you are really interested in this job, pick and choose the benefits or increases that you need. Do not just run the checklist of all of them at the same time.

If the company gets the sense that you are just interested in taking an offer to your current company in order to receive a counter offer, do not be surprised if they rescind theirs.

What a nice segue to the next chapter, "Resignation and the Temptation of the Counter Offer."

First, let's go through our checklist for the salary-negotiation process for people who are truly interested in the position.

JOB-SEARCH PROCESS CHECKLIST — Art of Salary Negotiation

❑ You continue to network until your first day on the new job.

❑ You review your list of "Wish I Would Have Saids" that you created after your interviews.

❑ When an offer is extended, the first thing you should do is tell them you are interested in the job and in working with them. Then you may either accept their offer if you are happy with it or ask if they have some flexibility in the offer.

❑ If they have some flexibility, ask if you can discuss your new information (Wish I Would Have Saids) that may impact their offer.

❑ Assure them that you are very interested in their position and working with them.

❑ It is important to negotiate your offer with them in a positive fashion. Do not take these negotiations personally.

❑ Discuss various options with them regarding increased base compensation, signing bonus, quarterly and annual bonuses, stock or stock options, increased vacation time, relocation benefits, etc.

❑ When you are happy with your negotiations, be prepared to accept their final offer immediately and commit to an agreed start date.

I hope the information presented here helps you in your negotiations! **Remain positive!** People do what you expect them to do. Good luck!

CHAPTER 8
RESIGNATION AND THE TEMPTATION
OF THE COUNTER OFFER

In Chapter 1, "Our First Steps Together," I discussed how our society values stability over change. Additionally, most people are uncomfortable with conflict; therefore, resigning from your current position can be very stressful. Few people find it easy to resign and really don't know how to end that professional relationship.

It is important to end your tenure at a company in a positive way. Remember, managers also change jobs. You never know if you will see one later in a new company.

Your resignation is actually a process — and some of you probably thought it was simply, "I quit."

The best way to resign is to write a resignation letter. It needs to be simple, positive and clear. It is also a way for you to avoid the initial potential conflict. Generally, managers will absorb the fact that you are resigning before coming to you to ask questions about your resignation.

This is a sample resignation letter:

Date

Dear *Manager* (obviously use their name):

I want to thank you for the time that I have spent working with you. It has been a time of personal and professional growth for me.

Company Name (your current employer) is a great company; however, I have received and accepted an offer to work with another company. This new position helps me further my professional goals, and I am looking forward to starting with them on (start date).

My last day with *Company Name* will be Friday, Month Day (two-weeks' notice). During the next two weeks, I will transition any uncompleted work to co-workers.

The decision to leave is a final decision for me. I have no interest in receiving a counter offer.

Sincerely,

(your signature)

John Doe

As you can see, the information is concise and positive. There is no need to share the name of your new employer.

When asked why you are leaving, simply say the new position is with a company that will give you the opportunity to grow and make new impacts — and that you are really looking forward to working with the new company. Your manager needs to know that you are happy with your decision to leave and will not consider a counter offer. Tell your manager if he has any transitional questions after your departure that you are willing to answer any of those questions.

If the manager pushes you to stay longer than two weeks to transition your work, remember any additional time in the position may be very painful when they pressure you to accept a counter offer — and they will pressure you almost daily. I've worked with candidates who called me in their third week. They were complaining to me that it was not about transitioning work. The company was pressuring them to stay. I suggested that the next day they announce, "The work is complete, so I am leaving at noon to start with my new company. It has been a pleasure working with you! Thank you!"

As your performance was measured during your tenure with that company, your performance as you depart will be measured and remembered. Make it as positive a memory as you can.

Emotions run high during the time when you resign. So there is no surprise when someone tells me they have decided to accept a counter offer within their own company.

Prior to accepting a counter offer, you should attempt to make it a rational decision rather than an emotional decision. Consider that recruiting industry newsletters like the *Fordyce Letter* track the percentages of people who accept counter offers and are still with their company six months to a year later. An amazing 80 percent of all people who accept a counter offer leave their current company within a year after accepting the counter offer to stay.

Think about that for a minute. Las Vegas was built and all of that electricity is paid for by people taking risks when the odds are against them; therefore, of every 1,000 accepted counter offers, only 200 people remain at their company a year later, while 800 of them have left (some of those not by their choice), usually within six months.

The 800 people who left must experience the stress of another job search — and usually have one fewer option since they have broken that trust. Because they were successful enough to receive an offer this time, they should be confident enough to succeed again. But there is no reason to believe the original position is still open — or if the company even would consider them as a candidate again. The original trust has now been broken by acceptance of the counter offer.

I worked with a candidate who was interested in a management position within a consulting company in the top-secret world. My client was a small boutique company within that world that had a great reputation with its clients. As a result, they were beginning to grow and needed to bring in a technically talented manager to help that growth succeed.

The candidate sailed through the interviews successfully. He had the perfect credentials for my client and the right attitude and skills to manage a small team. As a result of his interviews, the candidate received an offer from my client. When he resigned, his current company offered him a counter offer that matched his newly offered compensation from my client. More important, they offered him the opportunity to lead a team. Since he viewed himself as a loyal employee and his company appeared to match my client's offer, he accepted his company's counter offer.

My client was obviously very disappointed on a number of levels:

1. They thought their search for a new manager was over and that he would soon start.

2. Once they extended his offer and he accepted, they assumed their search was over and notified other candidates.

3. Now they were going to have to begin from scratch to search for a new qualified candidate within a very small community of potential candidates.

4. He had broken the trust and the commitment that he made to my client.

You can probably understand why my client did not want to hear his name later.

And later did come… After he accepted the counter offer, his manager told him that they would begin to expand in several months and that is when he would get the team to manage. As soon as his company heard that a new manager began at my client's company three months later, they told him that they were slowing down their expansion and he would not have a team to manage for the foreseeable future.

Of course, he did still have the extra compensation, but the reason he was looking initially was not money, it was the additional challenge of managing a team. Now he was unhappy again — and his own company broke that trust, again.

He immediately called me as soon as his manager gave him that news. "Was the position still available?" I told him that my client just had someone start in the position the day before.

Now he realized that his company had betrayed him and was more disappointed than before he began his first search. My client was not interested in hearing he was available because they felt he broke his commitment to them.

He found another position a short time later and left his company.

Why do managers and companies extend counter offers? There are many reasons:

- They really need a person to fill that role, and the current person did so nicely (and sometimes below market value, particularly if they have been a long-term employee).

- They also recognize no other current employee can fill that role.

- They suddenly recognize the value that person brings, particularly the knowledge of the position and potential competitive intelligence that person will take with them.

- The manager recognizes he will now need to conduct a search for a new employee and spend the time and money to train them.

- If they leave, someone else will need to perform those tasks until the position is filled by a new person and they are trained.

- Some people are poor managers. They may have already lost members of their team and are afraid how this next departure will impact their future as a manager.

- They are also afraid that this departure, particularly if the person is well liked, may trigger more employees to look for and find new positions.

- They are afraid of the impact of the employee's departure on morale.

- They are afraid of the impact of hiring someone new to their compensation structure, particularly if the current employee discovered the compensation was under market value.

Most of the time, concerns revolve around themselves and not their employee. These managers are struggling to maintain their grip on a person who stated they are leaving. Suddenly, an employee who was not so important has become a very important person (for a while).

Those are some of the reasons and fears of the manager and of the company. Why should an employee be wary of the counter offer?

- Now your manager and company know you are unhappy there. So a certain level of trust has been broken within your own company.

- What are your most important assets to your company now that they know you want to leave? Your knowledge of your position, processes, systems, people, etc. Some of this knowledge will not be replaced for a long time.

- If they offer you more money during the counter offer, are you setting yourself up to lose next year's raise?

- Why are you suddenly worth more today — after your resignation — than you were worth yesterday? Many people become upset when they consider this aspect.

- Is there a possibility your company will conduct a brain drain on you after you accept a counter offer? (They know the statistics as well!) Will they get the information they need from you and then replace you once a new person is up to speed?

- Remember, the foundation of behavioral interviewing? Once the manager feels that you are locked in, do you really believe that things will change? Probably not!

- Do you really believe them when they say they are happy you decided to stay? Are they happy for you, or happy for themselves? Now they have Old Reliable still in the seat and don't have to spend time and money to recruit a replacement.

- Remember the odds are against your success at your company after you resign from that company. They just want someone to do the job until they decide how to "protect themselves."

While I preach a good game on counter offers, it took two bad experiences for me to be convinced that accepting a counter offer is unwise. Both times I left within six months of the counter offer — the second time I was a successful recruiter and certainly should have known better.

I was a senior recruiter working with a noted contingent recruiting firm with offices in Washington, D.C., and New York City. As I was having success in the contingency world, I decided that I wanted to mentor and train my own team. There were some things that I would do differently than my manager.

After discussions with my manager/partner broke down, I discussed my candidacy with another firm in Maryland a little closer to my home. They made me an offer immediately that I accepted.

When I went back to my manager/partner and resigned, he was dumbfounded. He went on a full-court press to get me to stay, including putting me on a shuttle flight to New York City to visit with his partners. His partners wined and dined me and assured me that we would come to an agreement and I would be able to develop my own team. I returned that evening full of promise and decided to stay there. The other firm was very disappointed that I changed my mind.

Over the next couple of months, I focused primarily on my recruitment fee production while looking for the right talent to recruit. About the time I found someone to hire, the partner had hired someone else to grow his consulting business and told me that it was up to the new manager. The new manager told me that he wanted to go in another direction (consulting). The trust was broken. I left two weeks later.

I am still friendly with my manager/partner there. He acknowledged that he made a bad decision — and so did I. Once I decided to leave the first time, I should have left.

When you resign, what should you expect to hear from your company if they are going to extend a counter offer? Many times I list these statements for the candidates and ask them to tell me how many they hear. While this is an important time for the departing employee, companies are amazingly consistent in what they say to the person who wants to leave.

- "I am shocked that you want to leave. I thought you were happy. As a matter of fact, tomorrow we were going to discuss a (promotion, raise, new project, etc.) with you." (Call me a cynic, but the supposed timing is an amazing coincidence, wouldn't you agree?)

- "You are a very valuable employee. We need to see what we can do to encourage you to stay."

- "I am happy that you came to me because I planned to chat with you about moving to another organization in our company (that was nixed in a previous conversation weeks before)."

- "I am very disappointed that you chose such a busy time to leave our organization. Can't you see the impact your departure will have on everyone else?" (I love that one. The manager is trying to put a guilt trip on you.)

- "Your manager just came to me to discuss your resignation.

I asked if I could talk with you. You are a key person in our growth plans. I am sorry we haven't shared this with you sooner. Let's sit down and discuss the needed changes…" (Generally an executive speaking.)

- "What will it take for you to stay?" (At least that one is up front in its intent!)

- "As you know, we rarely give counter offers here, but you are such a key person, we will make an exception. What do you want to stay?"

- "Thank you for coming to me and discussing needed changes. Would you like to lead those changes?" (Generally, if you accept the counter offer, the desire to make immediate changes in the organization dissolves shortly after you accept.) Then they will say, "Let's just finish what you are working on first. Then we will discuss the changes." (Note, they won't say "make the changes" again.)

For your own satisfaction, track how many of these statements you hear when you resign.

My client extended an offer to a candidate who accepted the offer. We sat down. I chatted with him about the counter offer experience that I had personally. Then we discussed the statements that he might hear the next day when he resigned. I suggested that he track them and call me at the end of the day and let me know which ones he heard.

Sure enough, I received a call from him early in the evening after they had taken him to dinner (those wily devils!). He was laughing. They managed to hit seven out of eight statements. That's certainly better than average!

He honored his commitment and went to work with my client.

I have another counter offer story. In 1993, we were traveling across the country looking for candidates for a Midwestern city. One candidate I had interviewed received an offer. This is his story.

We extended the offer to this candidate and he accepted on the spot. He was very excited about his offer. On the Wednesday before he was leaving the company, his manager called him in and put him on the spot. He was great at putting employees on guilt trips, and this one worked. I received an e-mail from one of the managers I worked with saying that he accepted a counter offer. I asked the manager if he wanted me to try to "save" him. He replied, "Please!"

I called the candidate and asked if we could sit down for a soda on Saturday afternoon when I was back in town. He said, "Sure."

When we got together, we chatted for almost an hour over the soda discussing what had happened. When he was finished, I asked him if he was happy that he accepted the counter offer. He was undecided. I suggested that in my experience, when I make a decision that feels right, it seems the weight of the world has left my shoulders. I observed that, based on our chat, it appeared that weight was still there. Then I asked him if he would like me to tell him how to resign and still make orientation on Monday. He said, "Sure."

He told me that his manager generally was in on Mondays by 7 a.m. I told him to get there at 6:30 a.m. and empty his cubicle. When 7 a.m. rolled around, go to the manager and say, "Two weeks ago I turned in my notice. Last week you pressured me to stay. I didn't want to stay, but you pressured me, so I accepted your counter offer. After thinking it over during the weekend, I decided to honor my commitment and go to work for my new company. Here are my keys and identification. I need to run to make orientation." Then leave.

He asked me if he could take time to think about it. I said, "Sure, just let me know tomorrow if you want to be in orientation Monday morning so I can send a note to let them know to expect you. As promised, he called me on Sunday and told me he would be in orientation.

It's almost 20 years later, and he is still with my former client.

Bottom line — you made a commitment to your new manager. Honor your commitment.

JOB-SEARCH PROCESS CHECKLIST —
Resignation and the Temptation of the Counter Offer

❏ Write a simple, positive resignation letter.

❏ When asked why you are leaving, simply say the new position is with a company that will give you the opportunity to grow and make new impacts — and that you are really looking forward to working with the new company.

❏ Tell your manager that you are not interested and will not consider a counter offer.

❏ Assure the manager that you will ensure your work is transitioned to the team.

❏ If pushed to remain on the job longer than two weeks, carefully monitor progress on transitioning work. When the pressure to accept a counter offer is greater than the pressure to transition work, it is time to leave immediately.

❏ Read once more the odds against a successful tenure after accepting a counter offer.

❏ Understand the reasons why companies suddenly decide to extend a counter offer.

❏ Review the reasons why the employee should be wary of the counter offer.

❏ Count how many of the counter-offer-related statements you hear from managers and executives once the word gets out that you resigned.

❏ Once you accept an offer and give a start date, honor your commitment to start on that date.

This is a good time to discuss your first few weeks on the new job in Chapter Nine: "Your First Day on the Job!"

CHAPTER 9
YOUR FIRST DAY ON THE JOB!

Congratulations! Doesn't it feel good to have finally reached this point? Typically, you are experiencing a number of feelings now — elation, anticipation, excitement, enthusiasm and yes, even a little fear. As you have experienced, your job search turned out to be an emotional roller coaster ride and you are happy it's over.

As RecruiterGuy, may I suggest that while everything is fresh in your memory, it is time to prepare for your next search? Jot down what actions were successful for you during this search. What would you have done differently?

I totally understand that deep down you are hoping you will remain with this company for the balance of your career; however, the odds today work against that potential conclusion unless you are at the very end of your career.

Remember to thank everyone who helped you in your search and let them know where you are now working. Now that you have a business relationship, they may be a good source to contribute to solutions to problems that are confounding you, and you may be able to return the favor.

Continue to network with people to see how you can help them. Remember your experience as you went through the job-search process. If you receive a call from someone who is attempting to network the way to a new position, take the call. Without spending an inordinate amount of time, make suggestions to help them better focus their search. Remember, you now have a huge list of potential people they can use to network. Obviously, not everyone on your list is good for their search, but at least a few of them are. You may make a difference in the person's life.

Understand that some people are users. Remember the singer warming up? Me, me, me, me! Spend tiny amounts of time with them instead and focus on people who understand networking is a two-way street.

One hopes you made some new friends during this journey. Nurture those relationships. They need not involve social interaction. They can be a quick phone call or e-mail asking how the person is doing. Keep your information on LinkedIn up to date and check out their activities occasionally. You may be able to answer a quick question for them.

One of the areas that most people can improve is to track their impacts. You can review this information prior to your annual review with your manager or executive board. If you find yourself in another search, this information will be sitting in a file on your personal computer instead of needing to be dredged up. Managers don't always track your impacts well (as you probably discovered prior to your last move). Therefore, it is your responsibility to track them. As you work through your quarterly or annual reviews, it is good to bring impacts up for discussion. This is not bragging. It is reinforcing in your manager's mind the problems that you are helping them solve.

As you work with your new manager, come to agreement on three-month, six-month, nine-month and 12-month goals for you. This keeps you on track to fulfill the goals for the year. Ask your manager to introduce you to the people who you will need to interface with to accomplish the goals.

It is advisable to make this an annual practice with each manager. During your reviews, you can discuss the goals completed. It also is a good platform to use when you need your manager to introduce you to someone new inside the company or to a vendor in order to meet your goal.

During these discussions, develop agreement on opportunities you see for your group and the company. Keeping your focus on your goals and company goals is the best way to be viewed as a person who makes a difference within the company. Helping your manager accomplish goals while accomplishing your goals is the vehicle to being viewed as a team player. If you build consensus with others in your company, it also is a great way to grow respect.

Once you have some credibility (by meeting your goals) with your manager, your goal-review time is a great time to discuss your future career goals. If your manager has a mentor type of relationship with you, she can be a great person to help you position yourself for your next move.

Remember in Chapter Four, "Effective Networking to Your Next Position!," when I said networking can be a simple conversation that can benefit both sides? Doesn't this also work inside companies? You may not call it networking inside your company, but that's what it is. Effectively networking within your company is a great way to be more effective working with other staff and management in your company. Networking within your company with other managers is a way to move within your company to gain new experience and make new impacts without taking time to look for a new job in another company.

Remember the goal of having so much fun at work that at the end of the day you say, "Wow! This was so much fun that I can't believe today is already over — and they are paying me, too!" How do you reach that level of job satisfaction? You reach it by making positive, measurable impacts and having fun. Meet your goals and help others meet theirs.

As you are meeting your goals, look for dirty jobs that others are avoiding. In my experience these "dirty jobs" have such a reputation of being time traps or are such a pain to do that they develop the reputation of being a monster. Tackle one of those jobs at a time from a Lean process-improvement or Six Sigma focus that eliminates waste. What you may discover is that your fresh look at the task can help you make a suggestion that improves it to the level that other people don't mind doing it; or you eliminated waste and contributed directly to the bottom line. You also may decide to automate it so no one has to do it again. You may discover it has outlasted its usefulness. Of course, before discarding information or deleting a task, confirm with your manager that it no longer needs attention.

People who successfully clean up the dirty jobs and make them efficient are the ones who succeed within companies.

Do we need a checklist at the end of this book? This one is easy:

Make impacts and have fun!

APPENDIX A
RESUME ACTION VERBS AND PHRASES

These verbs and phrases can be used to create more interest in your resume. Once you are interviewing, some of your material on your resume will be the base of your interview. Prepare yourself for your interview by creating true stories that demonstrate the skills in your resume. Chapters 1, 2 and 3 discussed the steps to create an effective resume.

These verbs and phrases have been separated by level of position (executive job searches, experienced and sales job searches and entry-level job searches); but they are by no means mutually exclusive. Feel free to draw from each list as needed.

Obviously, every field has its own jargon, so this list is not totally complete. The purpose is to give you a start that will help you remember more specific action verbs that apply to your experience.

The convention in resume writing is to write your sentences in third person past tense as if you were describing someone else's experience, even your current experience, and then drop the pronouns. You will note that all of these verbs are written in past tense.

Executive Searches Action Verbs

Accelerated	Augmented	Charted
Achieved	Authored	Cleared
Acquired	Awarded	Closed
Added	Balanced	Coached
Administered	Built	Collaborated
Analyzed	Captured	Communicated
Appraised	Catapulted	Competed
Assimilated	Chaired	Compiled
Assumed	Challenged	Completed
Assured	Championed	Composed

Conceived
Conceptualized
Conducted
Consolidated
Consulted
Converted
Coordinated
Counseled
Created
Cut
Defined
Delivered
Deployed
Developed
Devised
Directed
Distinguished
Diversified
Divested
Downsized
Dreamed/Dreamt
Drove
Eliminated
Engaged
Engineered
Enhanced
Ensured
Established
Evaluated
Exceeded
Executed
Expanded
Experienced
Finalized
Financed
Finessed
Focused

Found
Founded
Funded
Generated
Grasped
Guided
Honed
Identified
Imagined
Immersed
Implemented
Improved
Increased
Indicated
Initiated
Instituted
Integrated
Interacted
Interfaced
Introduced
Invested
Launched
Led
Leveraged
Licensed
Linked
Loaned
Managed
Marketed
Maximized
Mentored
Merged
Modified
Motivated
Negotiated
Operated
Opposed

Optimized
Orchestrated
Organized
Outsourced
Oversaw
Partnered
Performed
Pioneered
Planned
Positioned
Possessed
Powered
Practiced
Prepared
Presided
Procured
Promoted
Proposed
Protected
Provided
Purchased
Raised
Realigned
Rebuilt
Received
Recognized
Recommended
Redesigned
Reduced
Refinanced
Refined
Regulated
Renegotiated
Reorganized
Repositioned
Represented
Retained

Researched   Sold   Transformed
Resolved   Solidified   Transitioned
Responded   Spearheaded   Translated
Restored   Streamlined   Utilized
Restructured   Strengthened   Ventilated
Revised   Stretched   Vetted
Saved   Supported   Warehoused
Secured   Sustained   Worked
Selected   Transferred

Executive Phrases

Assessed corporate financial structure
Asset-based lending facility
Asset management
Best practices
Business development
Business divestiture
Business transformation
Capital acquisition
Capital restructuring
Change management
Competitive product positioning
Continuous process improvement
Contract negotiations
Corporate startup
Corporate turnaround
Cost improvement
Cost rationalization
Created stakeholder value
Creditor negotiation
Crisis management
Disciplined execution
Due diligence
E-commerce licensing

Equity private placement
Expense efficiencies
Financial restructuring
Global strategies
High-performance organizations
Human capital
Improved bottom-line profitability
Improved customer experience
Improved employee engagement
Improved value proposition
Increased profitability by percentage
Key vendor contracts
Market penetration
Merger management
New product/service and technology launch
Operational readiness
Organizational alignment
Organizational efficiency
Pay for performance incentives
Positive liquidity
Pricing strategy
Quarterly earnings calls
Raised $X million in new venture funding
Reduced operating costs
Significant market opportunities
Strategic imperatives
Strategic leadership
Strategic planning
Successful IPO
Succession planning
Value creation strategies

Experienced Talent and Sales Searches Action Verbs

Accompanied	Bracketed	Conceived
Accomplished	Branded	Conceptualized
Accounted	Bound	Conducted
Acted	Bridged	Consolidated
Added	Briefed	Constructed
Addressed	Buffered	Consulted
Administered	Built	Contributed
Admitted	Calculated	Controlled
Advanced	Captured	Converted
Advised	Cared	Cooked
Advocated	Carried	Coordinated
Agreed	Certified	Counseled
Aligned	Chaired	Created
Allocated	Challenged	Customized
Analyzed	Championed	Cut
Applied	Changed	Danced
Assembled	Charted	Deciphered
Assessed	Clarified	Decreased
Assigned	Classified	Defined
Assimilated	Cleared	Delighted
Assisted	Closed	Delivered
Assumed	Coached	Demonstrated
Assured	Coded	Designed
Attained	Collaborated	Determined
Audited	Collected	Developed
Authored	Combined	Discovered
Awarded	Commanded	Dispatched
Badged	Compared	Displaced
Balanced	Compiled	Disposed
Based	Completed	Distinguished
Benchmarked	Composed	Distributed
Blended	Computerized	Diversified

Documented	Handled	Merged
Doubled/Tripled	Heated	Modified
Downsized	Hired	Monitored
Drafted	Identified	Motivated
Dreamed/Dreamt	Ignited	Moved
Drove	Imaged	Multiplied
Dug	Imagined	Networked
Employed	Immersed	Obtained
Enabled	Implemented	Offered
Endured	Improved	Opened
Engaged	Incorporated	Operated
Engineered	Increased	Opposed
Enhanced	Indicated	Optimized
Established	Initiated	Orchestrated
Estimated	Injected	Ordered
Evaluated	Integrated	Organized
Exceeded	Introduced	Outperformed
Expanded	Intubated	Packaged
Extracted	Invested	Participated
Facilitated	Joined	Performed
Finalized	Laminated	Piloted
Financed	Launched	Pioneered
Finessed	Leased	Planned
Forced	Led (not the metal	Pointed
Forecasted	"lead")	Posted
Found	Linked	Powered
Founded	Listened	Prepared
Functioned	Loaned	Presented
Gained	Located	Presided
Gathered	Maintained	Priced
Generated	Managed	Prioritized
Graded	Manufactured	Processed
Graduated	Marched	Procured
Grasped	Marketed	Produced
Grew	Mentored	Programmed
Guided	Merchandised	Promoted

Proposed	Retained	Stirred
Prospected	Returned	Stored
Proved	Revamped	Streamlined
Provided	Reviewed	Stretched
Published	Revised	Structured
Punctuated	Revitalized	Supervised
Purchased	Rezoned	Supported
Qualified	Rinsed	Sustained
Raised	Sampled	Targeted
Rationalized	Saved	Tasked
Reacted	Searched	Teamed
Reassessed	Scoured	Terminated
Rebuilt	Screened	Tested
Recognized	Secured	Tracked
Recommended	Selected	Trained
Recruited	Served	Transferred
Reduced	Shortened	Transitioned
Re-engineered	Simmered	Tuned
Reflected	Simplified	Turned
Remodeled	Simulated	Utilized
Removed	Skilled	Verified
Repaired	Sold	Warehoused
Reported	Sought	Weighed
Represented	Sourced	Willed
Researched	Specialized	Wrote
Restored	Spent	

Experienced Talent and Sales Phrases

Achieved ambitious goals
Best practices initiatives
Brand awareness
Client focused
Cohesive, cross-functional team
Cold calling
Compensation analysis

Consistently X percent of goal
Consultative selling
Continuous process improvement
Creative client sourcing
Customer penetration
Due diligence
Employee engagement
Exceeded expectations
Execution of concept
Grew territory revenues X percent
Improved client experience by...
Increased growth and profitability
Investment community
Key business metrics
Lead generation
Lean continuous improvement
Long-term company growth
Maintained high employee retention
Market research
Merger and acquisition
Mission critical
Outstanding performance
Performance metrics
Reduced employee attrition
Reported sales metrics
Sales pipeline development
Six Sigma
Solution-based selling
Strategic sales positioning
Strategy development
Working capital

Entry-Level Searches Action Verbs

Accomplished	Charted	Demonstrated
Accounted	Checked	Designed
Achieved	Clarified	Determined
Acquired	Classified	Developed
Acted	Cleared	Devised
Added	Closed	Discovered
Administered	Coached	Dispatched
Admitted	Coded	Displaced
Adopted	Collaborated	Distinguished
Advanced	Collected	Distributed
Advocated	Combined	Diversified
Agreed	Compared	Documented
Allocated	Compiled	Drafted
Analyzed	Completed	Drove
Applied	Composed	Dug
Assembled	Computerized	Elaborated
Assessed	Conceived	Emphasized
Assigned	Conducted	Employed
Assisted	Constructed	Endured
Assumed	Consulted	Engaged
Attained	Contributed	Engineered
Attended	Controlled	Enhanced
Authored	Converted	Ensured
Awarded	Cooked	Established
Balanced	Coordinated	Estimated
Branded	Corrected	Evaluated
Built	Counseled	Exceeded
Calculated	Created	Excelled
Capitalized	Customized	Executed
Captured	Cut	Expanded
Cared	Danced	Experienced
Carried	Dealt	Explored
Certified	Deciphered	Facilitated
Challenged	Decreased	Filed
Championed	Delighted	Financed
Changed	Delivered	Finessed

Filled	Invested	Presented
Filmed	Joined	Presided
Flew	Laminated	Prioritized
Followed	Launched	Processed
Forecasted	Learned	Produced
Formed	Led	Programmed
Found	Linked	Promoted
Founded	Listened	Proposed
Functioned	Managed	Prospected
Gained	Manned	Proved
Gathered	Marched	Provided
Generated	Marketed	Published
Graded	Modified	Punctuated
Graduated	Monitored	Purchased
Grasped	Motivated	Qualified
Grew	Moved	Raised
Guided	Multiplied	Reacted
Hired	Negotiated	Recognized
Identified	Obtained	Recommended
Imaged	Offered	Recorded
Imagined	Opened	Reduced
Immersed	Operated	Reflected
Implemented	Opposed	Remodeled
Improved	Optimized	Removed
Incorporated	Orchestrated	Repaired
Increased	Ordered	Reported
Indicated	Organized	Represented
Initiated	Outperformed	Required
Injected	Paid	Researched
Input	Participated	Responded
Instructed	Partnered	Restored
Integrated	Performed	Resulted
Interacted	Piloted	Returned
Interfaced	Planned	Rinsed
Interned	Pointed	Sampled
Interviewed	Posted	Saved
Introduced	Practiced	Scheduled
Intubated	Prepared	Scoured

Searched	Spoke	Tracked
Secured	Stirred	Trained
Selected	Stored	Transferred
Served	Streamlined	Transitioned
Serviced	Structured	Tuned
Shadowed	Studied	Turned
Shared	Submitted	Understood
Shortened	Suggested	Updated
Simmered	Summarized	Used
Simplified	Supervised	Utilized
Simulated	Supported	Verified
Sold	Sustained	Weighed
Sought	Targeted	Won
Sourced	Taught	Worked
Specialized	Teamed	Wrote
Spent	Timed	

Entry-Level Phrases

Achieved on-time project performance
Participated in (any leadership roles in college like sports/clubs/student government)
Conducted case study on...
Created consensus
Exceeded expectations
Fluent in (foreign languages)
Honor society
Improved customer experience
Learned new work cultures through...
Led team in...
Paid/contributed to college expenses
Participated in industry co-op program
Held part-time college jobs
Completed relevant coursework
Researched...
Strong work ethic as evidenced by...
Student member of (professional association)
Worked in

APPENDIX B
POTENTIAL INTERVIEW QUESTIONS

Entire books have been written that focus solely on interviewing and interviewing questions. The purpose here is not to write a book, but to prepare you for some questions that you may have to field.

Obviously, every interview for every position in every company should be different; however, there are some general questions that may be asked at each level based on that level of experience and responsibility. Most of those questions probably will be self-explanatory. But after some questions, I will explain the motivation behind the question.

Review Chapter 6, "Impressive Interviewing," to see how these different methods of interviewing within the different interviewing formats may be used. Remember the value in telling stories to illustrate your experience and points.

These potential questions are separated by level of experience. Remember, most people conduct interviews without having been trained; therefore, even an executive may be asked a question that targets more junior-level experience because the interviewer may just be going down a list of questions that was handed to her by human resources or a friend. But, many questions are developed based on the challenges the candidate will face in the new position.

Some of the questions listed here were taken from actual interviews I have conducted. You can see that I have worked with a wide variety of people.

Use these questions to begin your interview preparation. It is not an exhaustive list, but should get you thinking in the proper frame of mind.

Executive-Level Questions

Based on my experience as a recruiter, just when you say, "They will never ask me a question like that. I'm too senior," some interviewer will ask you that question or one like it. Be prepared.

Describe your rise from the staff level to the executive level. What elements do you feel made the difference in your rise to executive level? Where was luck made?

How do you prepare yourself prior to starting as the leader of a new company?

Do you feel that working in one industry your entire career is more important than successfully working in several industries? Why/why not?

In your current/last position, what do you feel was the most important impact that you made? Why?

What was the most important impact that you made for the investors?

What challenges did you have to overcome? As a result of that experience, what did you learn?

Given your understanding of this position and the skills required to be successful, how do you feel your experience may differentiate you from other potential candidates?

Using 20/20 hindsight, describe an executive decision that you would have changed had you known then what you know now. *(Ask what level of detail they are looking for. Then tell the story at that level of depth.)*

A leader in a startup has a different role than a leader in a large, mature company or a leader in a corporate restructuring/turnaround. Compare and contrast the different roles these leaders have. Which roles have you filled? Of those roles, which do you prefer? Why?

If you are the leader of a pre-IPO startup, when do you decide to go on the road show to attract new funding? What elements do you feel need to be in place prior to your road show? Who accompanies you on this road show and what are their roles? What is your primary role?

Describe your corporate crisis management experience.

If you are the incoming president/CEO/CFO of a distressed company, what does your first day look like? First week? First month?

What reports do you want to see first? Why?

How often do you communicate with your board the first week and month? When are you confident that you can communicate less often?

Based on your experience and looking forward to the next five years, what situations do you feel would be ideal for you? Why?

There is a lot of talk today about improved productivity among your employees. How do you measure employee engagement? Based on your experience, describe how you improved employee engagement in your last position.

Which industries do you feel can be more profitable in these economic times? Based on your research on our company, what do you feel may be the low-hanging fruit that you will examine first? *(Those questions may be asked in any economic time.)*

What are the sales and marketing roles of the executives in a company this size?

When do you decide to make changes in the sales and marketing leadership roles within your company? Have you changed direction in the past? Were you happy with the result? What did you learn?

When you begin to lead a new company, what legal reports do you want to see first? Have you ever been surprised to find legal problems in a new company? Describe that experience. What did you learn from that experience?

What do you feel is the role of continuous improvement in our industry? Do you feel this company will benefit by instituting a formal continuous improvement program? What pushback do you expect from the current staff?

What do you feel are your best leadership skills? Why? Of those skills, which do you feel will serve you best in this position?

What skills will you need to improve while in this position? What process will you use to improve those skills?

When you are interviewing new members for your team, what do you feel is more important — skill or fit? Why?

How highly do you value human resources in your company? Does your human resource leader meet with your board?

What contribution to the company do you expect from your human resource leadership? Why? Does your current human resource department make that contribution? Why/why not?

What will former executive team members say about their experience working with you? Why?

In what areas do you feel they may suggest you need additional coaching? Why?

What do you feel is the hallmark of your success so far? Why? *(Great time for a story!)*

Obviously these are general questions that may be asked. You will hear more specific questions based on the needs of the company. The purpose of this list of questions is to help you think about the interview ahead of time.

Experienced and Sales-Level Questions

Tell me about your experience. *(This question may also be posed as, "Tell me about you." This is a great time to use your "Here I Am!" speech that you created in Chapter 2.)*

What was your last salary? What are you seeking? *(Essentially, both are the same question — trying to determine where you fit within their salary ranges. Remember your salary negotiation script in Chapter 7? This is an appropriate time to use it.)*

What training have you received from your current employer?

What training have you done on your own? *(Looking to see if you are passionate about what you do.)*

What professional association(s) do you belong to? Does your company pay the dues or do you pay them? *(If you only will belong to an association if your employer pays the dues, how serious are you about your profession?)*

Why are you interested in changing jobs at this time?

What do you like about your current position?

What annoys you at your current company? *(Be careful with your response to this question.)*

Have you ever had a confrontation with a co-worker? Describe the situation. What were your actions? How was the situation resolved?

Typically at what level of management do you interact?

How do you establish/maintain strong working relationships with company management?

How do you establish/maintain strong working relationships with your peers?

What do you find most helpful in a manager? Least helpful? *(The interviewer should know the style of management of the hiring manager. If your work style and your new manager's work style clash, it will be a poor match for both of you. Be honest.)*

Describe your idea of the best next job for you. *(Be honest. If you say what you feel the manager wants to hear, you may get a job you hate. It's better to know prior to an offer.)*

How does that fit within your long-term goals? *(Actually, they're trying to see if you set goals. Have you thought out where you want your career to head?)*

At what age did you begin to earn money for doing work? *(This could be babysitting or grass cutting.)* Why? *(Work ethic is established early. They are trying to determine your work ethic.)*

In your annual reviews, in what areas do you typically "Exceed Expectations"? Why?

In what areas do you typically fall short of expectations or only meet expectations? Why?

For positions that require driving
(such as sales, consulting or for-hire drivers)

Do you have a valid driver's license?

Have you ever had your driver's license suspended or revoked? Describe the situation. When was your license reinstated? *(It's best to respond honestly to this question. It's too easy to check during a background investigation. Many insurance companies will not allow employees to drive for business who have poor driving records.)*

For positions that require travel
(consulting, sales, marketing, driving long distances, etc.)

Have you ever traveled more than 50 percent of the time?

Is there anything that would prevent you from traveling overnight more than 50 percent of the time?

What do you like about business travel?

What percentage of overnight travel is acceptable to you?

Technical types of questions
(Obviously, a good manager will test your specific technical skills more strenuously!)

Describe your (data network/JD Edwards Development/Oracle applications/desktop support/web coordinator) experience.

What process do you use to troubleshoot technical problems? *(Looking for a step-by-step analysis.)*

What has been your biggest technical challenge? Describe the situation. What were your actions? What were the results? Why was this challenge different than other technical challenges?

What steps do you take to work with an internal client who is upset with the technology or the time to get a new system debugged?

What do you feel are your top five technical strengths with (specific technology)?

What technical skills do you feel you need to improve? How do you plan to improve those skills?

What training has your current employer given you?

Have you ever had to work with users spread out in different states? How did you support the remote internal clients?

Describe your process to develop credibility with your users when you begin working in a new position or area.

Within your area of expertise, where do you experience the most stress? How do you handle that stress?

Currently, what percentage of your time is spent doing new development vs. maintenance of older systems?

Marketing Questions

Why do you enjoy marketing?

How do you feel sales and marketing feed off of each other?

Do you feel it is helpful for a marketing professional to have sales experience? Do you have sales experience? Discuss your experience.

Discuss your brand-development experience.

Discuss your brand-development experience at the channel level.

Have you traveled to clients to learn how to help them make their sales goals with your product (pull-through selling)?

How do you bring value to your company's clients?

Describe your approach to potential clients.

Describe how you developed a marketing-support program.

Have you been a key contributor in the design and implementation of merchandising centers? Discuss one successful implementation.

Discuss your experience in the fulfillment center for the merchandising centers.

What are the key elements in a channel marketing program?

What tasks would you rather other people do in marketing?

Describe the skills and attributes of the perfect vice president of marketing to lead you.

How do you track the success of marketing efforts?

Sales Questions

What was your total compensation? What was your base? What was your commission or bonus? *(Sales professionals are the one group where I feel compensation should be shared. In my 29 years of recruitment experience, a sales professional typically earns what they believe they can earn. Most sales professionals earn roughly the same amount year after year, adjusted for inflation, unless there has been some life/work-changing event.)*

What percentage of goal/quota have you made for each of the last four years?

What really turns you on about the sales profession?

What would you rather have someone else handle for you?

How has automation changed your tracking of sales metrics?

Discuss a recent difficult sale that you closed. Why was it unusual? How did you finally close the sale? Is the client currently happy?

How do you normally source for new clients? Describe a recent effort. What was successful? What sourcing effort would you have preferred to be more productive?

While you are conducting needs analysis for a potential client, when are you convinced your solution is the best available?

What do you feel was your best sale? Why?

Describe some of the closes that you have successfully used. Which close has consistently been the most successful?

How do you keep your sales techniques fresh?

What practices do you use to maintain a positive mental attitude?

Describe how you set your goals. For you, what elements are included in a goal?

When do you plan for the week ahead?

How do you plan your day? Week? Month?

How do you define pull-through sales?

Explain the difference between one-step and two-step distribution.

Have you had success in the conceptual sales world? Describe your success. How does conceptual sales differ from product sales?

How do you bring value to your clients?

Describe a creative way you have approached potential clients.

How do you track the success of your efforts in the early months of new business development?

Describe how you were creative in accommodating a difficult client.

Project Manager Questions

What do you feel are your strongest project-management skills?

How would previous managers describe your project-management skills?

How will your current manager describe your organizational skills?

Many times, in order to get our jobs done, we are dependent upon others to do their jobs. Give me an example of a time when one of your peers did not have the same priorities as you and was not doing their part. How did you handle that situation? What was the final result?

What tool(s) do you use to track project progress?

How do you assign priorities when you are responsible for several projects?

Describe your most difficult project-management assignment. What did you learn from that experience? Have you dealt with a similar experience since?

How do you measure the success of a project? (*They are looking for on-time and/or under-budget project that meets requirements.*)

Accounting/Audit Questions

What area of accounting is your strength?

Why do you enjoy the accounting profession? (*Looking for impacts that can be made.*)

Discuss your experience with managerial accounting analysis and reporting.

How strong are your spreadsheet skills? Can you set up a spreadsheet and massage data?

Tell me your experience with standard costs/general ledger/accounts receivable or payable/payroll.

Have you been responsible for manufacturing cost analysis?

Have you been responsible for providing insight for areas of under-performance?

Have you provided sales pricing support for products or services?

Do you have an annual continuous improvement process for standards, inventory and reporting?

Do you have experience with reclaim valuation?

Are you comfortable working and interacting with senior management?

Give an example of a time when you had to convey negative news to senior management. How did you handle it in order to minimize defensiveness and arrive at the best way to remediate?

Describe your group's audit process.

In your current company, how long was your average audit in terms of days/weeks/months?

What percentage of your time is spent in compliance audits, financial audits, operational audits and systems audits?

What audit engagement taught you a valuable lesson? Describe the situation, your action and the results.

Construction Questions

Have you worked on any infrastructure or commercial or industrial construction sites? What were your responsibilities?

Do you have current safety certifications?

What reporting responsibility did you have on a construction site?

Have you ever worked on a wind farm or other renewable-energy construction site? If so, discuss your experience.

What situation best describes your problem-solving skills on a construction site? How was it received by management and other contractors?

How do you initiate and manage change on a construction site?

When you spot work habits that are unsafe, how do you handle the situation?

Describe a situation that was getting out of hand on a construction site. How did you handle it?

How do you convince the person who manages you that you have a better way of doing something? Describe a situation when you used that solution.

What do you feel are your construction management strengths?

What situation best demonstrates your leadership skills on a construction site?

What was the most unusual construction situation that you faced? How did you handle it?

How do you prepare yourself prior to starting on a new construction site?

Have you performed safety audits and, as a result, developed new safety programs or policies?

What do you feel you need to learn in order to be more credible with subcontractors on the construction site? How do you plan to improve those skills?

Human Resource Questions

Describe your experience working in a human resource department.

Typically, what was your most difficult task in human resources? Why?

Describe what you feel are the elements of a human resource business partner. What experience do you need to be a successful business partner? What are you doing to improve those skills?

What training has your company given you to improve your human resource skills?

What human resource training have you sought and paid for on your own?

Do you belong to the Society for Human Resource Management (SHRM)? Does your company pay for your membership? *(Trying to gauge your passion for your profession.)*

What is your process to entertain new ideas to improve human resource processes?

Tell me about a challenging employee issue that you had to handle. Discuss the situation. What were your actions? What was the result? What did you learn?

Discuss a manager who was difficult regarding an issue. Discuss the situation. What were your actions? What did you learn?

Describe the worst employee-relations issue that you had to handle. What was the result? Do you feel you handled it in the best possible way? What did you learn?

Discuss your human resource strategy development process for this year. What areas needed process improvement?

Discuss a time when you needed to sell senior managers on a new, more expensive (initially) program to improve the business.

Professionally, what would you do a different way if you were given an opportunity to do so? Why?

Discuss a benefits program you introduced that was praised by the employees and saved your company money?

How do you measure employee engagement? How have you improved employee engagement at your current employer?

What element do you feel was most effective in increasing employee engagement?

How did you measure the increase in employee engagement? Who suggested those metrics?

What is your experience in talent acquisition/recruitment? Discuss a situation in which you attracted an impact performer and saved your employer money in the process? *(There are many differing metrics being used here, including integrity.)*

What was your most creative way to source and hire an important employee? How did you decide to employ that process?

In detail, describe the different processes involved in the successful recruitment process.

What applicant tracking/HRIS have you used? Which system do you feel is the best?

Have you successfully sourced candidates through the corporate applicant-tracking system? What do you like about your system? What do you dislike?

What recruitment marketing suggestions have you made for your corporate web site?

Discuss how you best utilize the talents of a third-party recruiter. What do you feel are the challenges of working with a third-party recruiter?

When we do our reference check, how will the managers that you support describe their experience working with you? Why do you feel we will get that response?

What is your level of compensation analysis experience? Describe the projects that you have completed in this area.

In our reference check, how will your manager describe your strengths and areas of required improvement?

Entry-Level Questions

Have you participated in any internships in college?

What was your first internship?

Describe your experience. What kinds of responsibilities did you have?

What did you learn?

What was your biggest adjustment?

What steps did you take to gain acceptance from the full-time staff?

Did they ask you to return for a second internship or offer you a job after graduation?

Would you like to work at that company again as a full-time employee? Why/why not?

Did you work part-time during college? Where?

If so, why?

What did you learn?

What benefits do you feel you gained as a result of your work experience?

What experience in college or work do you feel relates to the skills needed to be successful in this position? *(This is a great time to relate a story about your experience that demonstrates your skills.)*

Did you participate in extracurricular activities in college? Which ones? Why did you pick them?

Did any of your extracurricular activities give you the opportunity to work with a team of other students or professors? What did you learn about working as a team member?

How do you feel you contributed to each of those activities (leadership, ideas, participation in events)?

What would you have done differently?

How do you feel your extracurricular activities affected your GPA? Looking back, would you have made different choices? Why/why not?

Did you work in high school? Why? *(Work ethic is developed early. This question is trying to determine whether you worked because your parents forced it on you, or you wanted to work for the monetary independence it gave you.)*

When we ask the manager about your work in your high school part-time job, what do you think she will say about your work and work ethic? Have you asked for a reference for other jobs or your college application?

What will the manager(s) say about their work experience with you during your summer jobs/internships?

Which professors do you feel would be good references to discuss your work ethic in college? Why?

What do you feel they will say to us during a reference check?

How do you feel that college prepared you for this position?

Which courses/experiences specifically prepared you for this job?

We realize that few college graduates will move right into a position without needing additional training. After reading the job description, where do you feel we will need to provide you with additional training?

Rate yourself on a scale of 1 to 10 (10 being an experienced Microsoft Office Developer) as a Microsoft Word user. Excel? PowerPoint? Access? How will other classmates rate your experience? How will professors rate you? How will you be rated when we discuss this rating with managers you reported to? *(Hint: Don't rate yourself too highly. Otherwise, you will not be able to meet expectations. Give a brutally honest appraisal after asking the interviewer what a 10 looks like — and tell the interviewer why you rated yourself at this level.)*

Discuss a successful experience that you had while working. Why do you feel it was successful? *(Here is your opportunity to use a story that you developed in the early chapters of this book.)* What did you learn from this experience?

Everyone makes mistakes. What mistake did you make that taught you a valuable lesson? Describe the situation, your actions and the result. What would you do differently next time? *(This question is asked to measure your honesty. If you truly never made a mistake, it's time to call the Pope to get you on the fast track to sainthood!)*

Where do you want to make impacts immediately? What experience do you have that will enable you to make those impacts?

Why do you want to work at our company? *(You have been coached to research companies prior to your interview. Companies are aware of that coaching. Now they are testing whether you accept coaching.)*

Have you been in a confrontation with a fellow student? Discuss the situation, how you handled it, and the result. What did you learn from the situation?

You can use these questions, or some form of them, in the future when you find yourself interviewing candidates for an opening that you are recruiting.

Good luck in your next job!